Boulder, CO

This books belongs to:

_____

THE THINKER'S TOOLBOX:
Mastering Decisions Workbook
for Teens & Tweens

Boulder, CO

Introduction, or Why You Should Think About Flies

Imagine this: you're preparing for an exam. A fat, juicy fly flies in through the cracked-open window and starts buzzing loudly around the room. Your focus immediately shifts.

What should you do? While you're thinking, the insect lands on your apple—one you've already bitten into! Oh no! What germs do flies carry? You'll need to look this information up. But how can you know what to trust on the internet?

What else could the fly have affected? The objects it has touched? Your mood? Your readiness for tomorrow's exam? If everything in the world is interconnected, are you and the fly elements of the same system? Argh!

The fly continues to drone persistently around the room. How can you catch it? Maybe you could think up a totally new approach. What if you started a business and called it "Fly Fighters"? That's right, you need a creative idea... and then a strategy too.

There's so much to think about. Is it worth stressing over? Of course not. After all, it's just a fly. But...

What if, instead of a fly, a more serious matter entered your life? For example, finding a good tutor or choosing a profession. That's when you'll definitely need to engage your thinking—critical, strategic, creative, and systemic. And how exactly do you do that? You'll learn in this workbook.

Between these covers, you won't find traditional exercises with objectively correct answers. Instead, you'll be invited to experiment, tune into your creativity, and test what you've learned. You can complete this workbook on your own or with others—your friends or parents. All you'll need is a writing utensil and to be sharp as a hawk. You definitely have a writing utensil. If you're wondering what it means to be "sharp as a hawk" and if you've got it—keep reading, and you'll find out.

You'll also discover how your brain processes information and how to verify its reliability; whether you can become an expert and persuade others; how to learn things that are important and useful; how to choose a profession and view the present day from a future perspective; how much creativity you have and how your imagination can become your education and problem-solving's best friend.

You're not thinking about that fly anymore, are you? Good. It's time to get started.

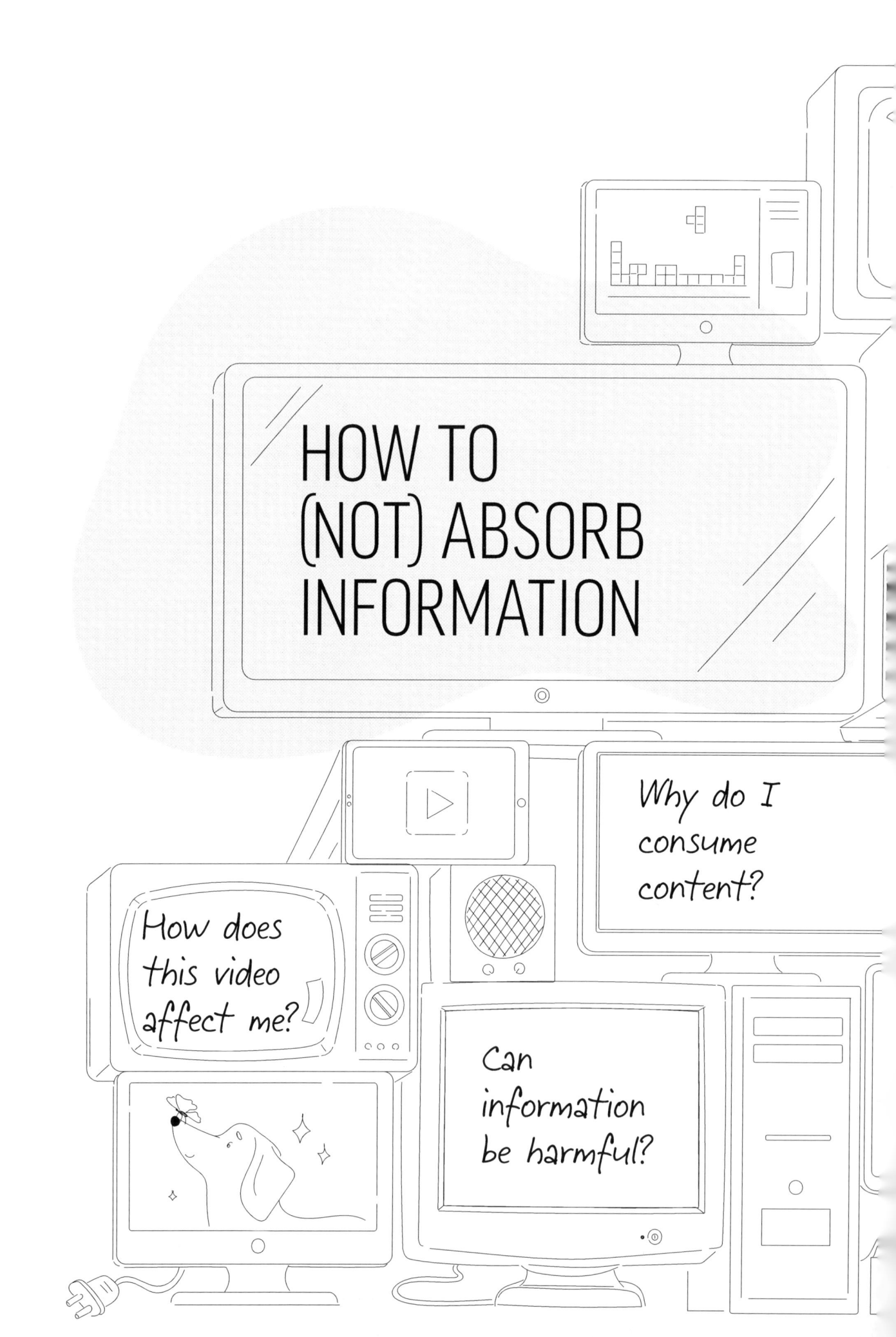

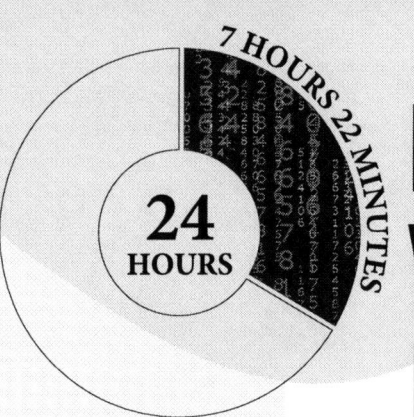

HOW AND WHY DO I SEEK INFORMATION?

By the way, this is a fact. But you can verify its accuracy yourself.

You'll learn about what constitutes facts and why it's important to verify them in the chapter on critical thinking.

Researchers have found that today's teens spend an average of 7 hours and 22 minutes online each day. Out of this time, a significant 3 hours and 28 minutes are dedicated to social media.

And how much time do you spend surfing the web?

◯ The same amount.
◯ Even more.
◯ Less... I think.

Color it in on the diagram!

The internet is the most expansive source of information available today. You can find anything online.

Well, almost anything. Are you always able to find what you're interested in?

◯ Always.   ◯ Almost always.   ◯ Rarely.

Being able to search for information is one of the most essential skills of the 21st century.

Do you usually find the information, or does the information find you?

"Ads on social media drive me crazy. You're scrolling through your feed, looking at photos or videos, and then—bam!—there's an ad, and it takes me a second to realize it's an ad! Plus, they keep showing things similar to what I've liked before. How do they even find me?"
(Savva, 14 years old)

8

What is Information?

Everything around you becomes information for your brain—objects, colors, sounds, textures, and tastes. You absorb information through all your senses, whether it comes from your environment or from a glowing screen. Your brain continuously processes and transforms this information—into what?

The information around me	Turns into…
Text from a textbook	New knowledge
Videos on social media	Intense emotions
Advertisements	The desire to buy something
Grades in school	Beliefs about abilities
Messages from friends	----
World news	----
My cat's purring	----
XP in a video game	----
----	----
----	----
----	----
----	----

After this type of processing occurs, information becomes a part of you—your memories, perceptions, emotions, desires, habits, and views.

Sometimes, in our pursuit of pleasure, we are willing to "binge" on tons of various and not always beneficial information. And sometimes, during aimless scrolling, we can run into something unpleasant or even harmful to our emotional well-being.

"Recently, I watched a video of a fight on social media. It looked like some guy was being beaten up, and they were even filming it on their phones. It made my skin crawl. Suddenly I started feeling sort-of afraid and disgusted…"
(Marina, 15 years old)

(Un)Helpful Information

The information you consume can be compared to food. Try dividing this plate based on the type of information you feed your brain the most.

Not all the information we ingest leaves a good aftertaste. Sometimes, it's just the opposite. Does that sound familiar?

The internet is overflowing with information for every taste, just like a buffet spread.

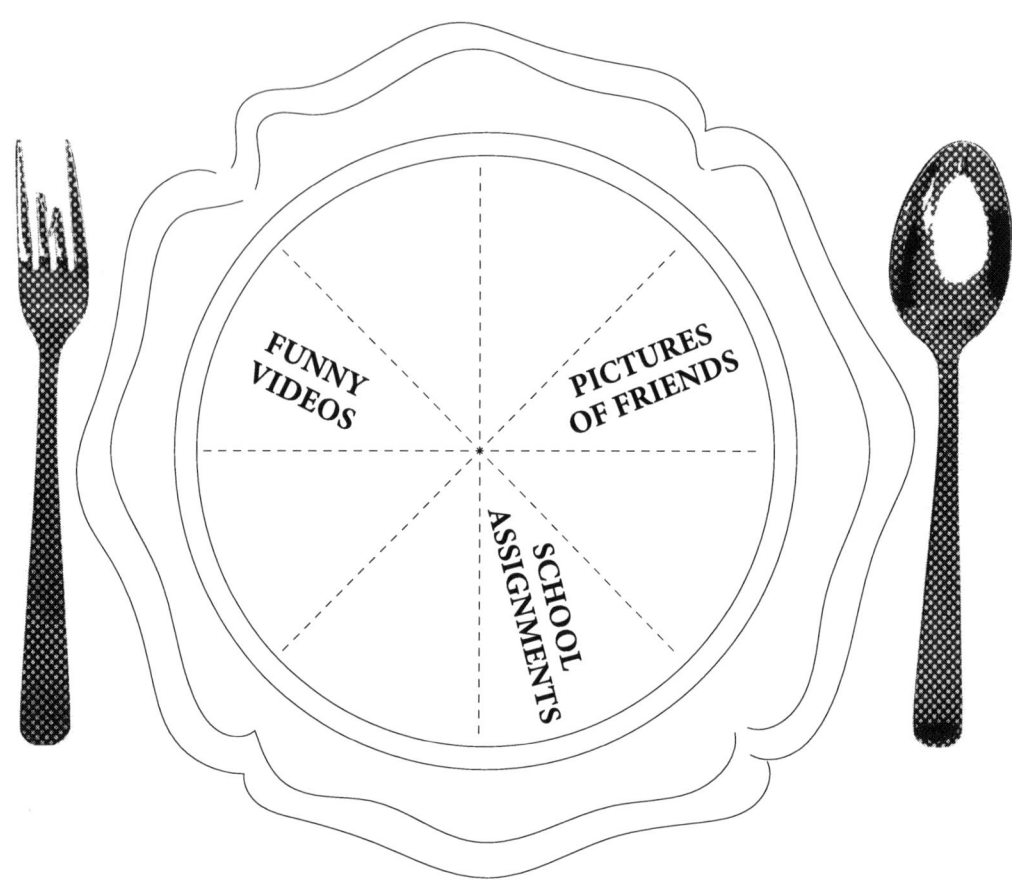

Take a closer look at your "information plate." What do you consume the most, and what value does it hold for you? Is it easy for your brain to digest this kind of information?

Write down your thoughts so you don't forget them.

_____

_____

_____

_____

Not everything that's easily digestible is good for you. Sometimes, the most dangerous things are those that slip into your mind unnoticed or seem perfectly harmless at first.

To avoid being hurt by information, it's crucial to know when it's helpful ☺, when it's neutral 😐, and when it can be harmful 😵 (at least to your mental health).

What I watch, read, or listen to...

	☺	😐	😵
Helps me learn or work better.	☐	☐	☐
Gets in the way of my learning or work.	☐	☐	☐
Doesn't affect my studies or work.	☐	☐	☐
Puts me in a good mood.	☐	☐	☐
Causes me unpleasant feelings (fear, anxiety, guilt, shame).	☐	☐	☐
Doesn't make me feel any strong emotions.	☐	☐	☐
Doesn't take time away from other important things.	☐	☐	☐
Takes all my attention and leaves no time for other important stuff.	☐	☐	☐
Helps me wind down and recharge.	☐	☐	☐
Makes me feel tired and drained.	☐	☐	☐

Managing information is like managing your diet: don't overindulge. Even the most useful information can have a negative effect if you consume too much of it. At the very least, you might feel tired. But at worst?

To avoid the nasty side effects of informational "overeating," it's important to know how to find the info you actually need.

Different people react to the same information in varying ways.

To figure out how it affects you, listen to your emotions, keep an eye on your overall well-being, and note any changes going on inside you.

How, Where, and What to Search For

You can set out to find information deliberately. Other times, you might just bump into it accidentally—more on that in the next section. But for now, let's dive into the best ways to find exactly what you need.

Think back to what you've combed the web for recently. Maybe it was a book, a catchy song, game reviews, a coding example, a recipe, a video tutorial, or advice from an expert.

Are you trying to find the best gluten-free rhubarb pie recipe or tips to become a world-class Irish dancer? There can be no route without a **destination.**

What am I looking for?
Jot down your objective.

Any info you're looking for is out there somewhere—whether it's in books, blogs, social media, or even in someone else's brain.

Where might I find it?
List all the places where this info might be hiding.

A great researcher, analyst, or detective always plans ahead: what, where, and how they're going to search. They rely on critical thinking, strategic planning, and a systematic approach to get the job done right!

How can I find it?
Write out the ways you can find those sources.

If you can nail down these three questions, you'll have a solid search plan that keeps you from going on wild goose chases or being sidetracked by distractions. Especially if you're searching for something online.

Search Strategies

As the saying goes, "First time's the charm!"
Now wait a second…

It's hardest to find what you need when:

- ◯ You don't know what you're looking for;
- ◯ You don't know where to look;
- ◯ You don't know how to look for it.

I don't know what I'm looking for

"Sometimes I feel like watching a movie in the evening, but I can't decide which one. I never get around to finding something interesting." (Katie, 14 years old)

"At school, we were asked to pick our own ecology topic and write an essay about it. It needs to cover research and include examples. But I don't even know where to start until I settle on a topic." (Ivan, 16 years old)

What would you suggest to Katie?

- ◯ To figure out what genre or type of movie she wants to watch first, and then look for films in those categories or use keywords to narrow it down.
- ◯ To start scrolling through all the movies suggested to her—maybe one will catch her eye.

The second strategy works if you have broad interests and plenty of free time. But if you already know what you're interested in and want to avoid wasting time, the first strategy will be way more effective.

What advice would you give to Ivan?

- ◯ To pick a topic or a range of topics, and then go on a focused search using keywords related to that topic.
- ◯ To search for any information related to ecology, and then figure out a specific topic as he goes.

Starting with a clear goal will save you time right off the bat. But if you're not quite sure what you need, kick things off with more general questions. As you dig in, the target will become clear to you and you can zero in on the specifics.

Without a clear goal in mind, you're unlikely to find what you're looking for. Plus, you'll end up wasting a ton of time.

Your goal might change during your search. At first, you might be looking for one thing, but then you stumble upon something even more interesting and find yourself wanting to learn more about that instead!

Still, it's crucial to keep a clear goal in mind. With your eyes on the prize, you'll stay focused and be less susceptible to distractions.

What if you knew of a long-lost treasure but had no clue where it was located? That's what having a search goal without understanding where to look is like. As a pirate would say, "Argh!"

AI stands for Artificial Intelligence.

I don't know where to look

"I want to find a remote design job. I love drawing and could make money doing it. But I'm not really sure where to look for that kind of job." (Chris, 17 years old)

If you're not sure where to find what you need, don't just stick to the internet. Check out these other options, too:

- ☐ Ask someone else—like your friends, parents, teachers, or anyone who might know where to find the information you need.
- ☐ Head to a bookstore or library and flip through books on the topic you're interested in. You can take photos of covers or pages you find useful, and then search for those books online later. And if you come across a book you really like, why not grab a copy for yourself?
- ☐ Consult an expert—someone who specializes in the topic you're interested in. You can find them in your circle, but also don't be shy about reaching out over social media!

If you're still having trouble finding what you're looking for, it might be time to tweak your goal. If you can't find an article for your essay on your chosen topic, consider adjusting the topic a bit or setting a new search goal.

I don't know how to look for it

Sometimes the issue isn't a lack of tools, but not knowing how to employ them. What search skills do you usually use?

- ☐ I identify keywords and search with them.
- ☐ I use hashtags to find things on social media.
- ☐ I know how to pose the right questions to AI.
- ☐ I'm skilled at asking people questions and conducting conversations.
- ☐ I can navigate online courses effectively.
- ☐ I'm able to read large texts both quickly and carefully.
- ☐ I speak more than one language, so I can read and listen in several.

You might find the information you need but struggle with understanding it. It happens. Seek out help from someone who can break things down for you. They might not even be human—a chat with an AI could clear things up just as well!

Should I ask AI?

An AI chat is a double-edged sword: It's dedicated to getting you the information you need at any cost. If it can't find it, it will fabricate it. It might stick to solid facts... or cleverly mislead you.

Which of these tips should you follow when searching for information?

	👌	👎
Ask clear, specific questions and give step-by-step instructions.	☐	☐
Request that AI confirms information with source links.	☐	☐
Cross-check the information AI provides with other sources.	☐	☐
Don't share too much personal info with AI.	☐	☐
Use AI as a tool, not as a replacement for your own thinking.	☐	☐
Ask AI to do all the mental work for you.	☐	☐
Treat AI as the hands-down best resource out there.	☐	☐

You can supplement these tips with your own!

_ ☐ ☐

_ ☐ ☐

_ ☐ ☐

_ ☐ ☐

Psst... Some of these tips were actually written by AI. Do you have any idea which ones?

If we offload all our thinking to AI, how are we supposed to have a mind of our own?

And this book is exactly for learning how to think not just independently, but also effectively in any situation.

AI can whip up any informational dish that you order. But do you know where it gets its ingredients, and if they're all safe to consume?

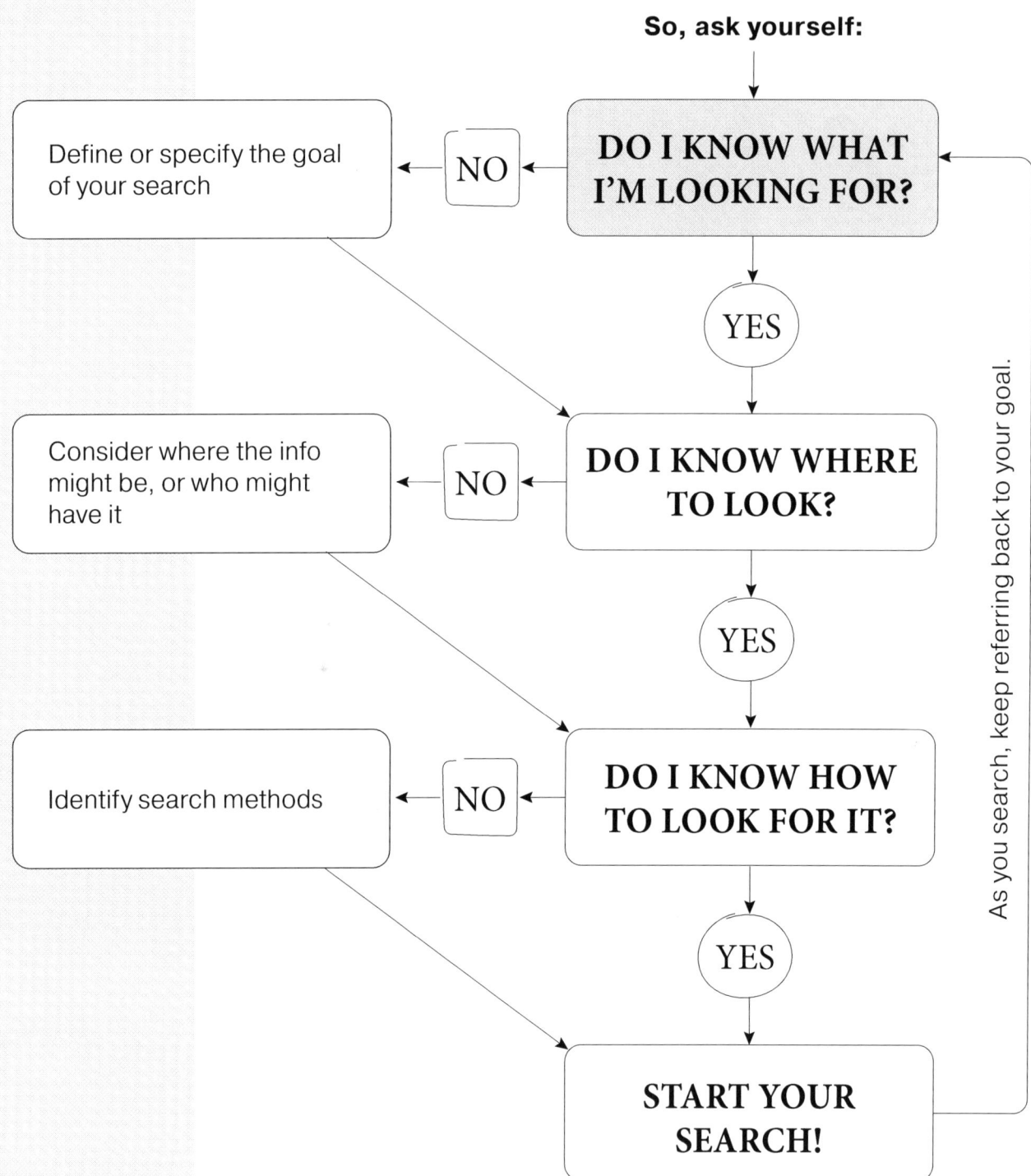

I'd also like to learn how to:

- [ ] eliminate distractions and stay focused;
- [ ] verify the accuracy of information and its sources;
- [ ] determine if an expert is trustworthy;
- [ ] find facts and see through lies.

In the other sections, we'll cover all this and more!

HOW AND WHY DOES INFORMATION FIND ME?

In today's world, there's so much information that you need to be skilled not just at finding it, but also at avoiding it! Especially when unwanted information won't stop chasing after you.

Think that doesn't happen?

○ It does!

○ It hasn't happened to me...

Open up your feed, scroll through it, and check out how many text posts, videos, or photos pop up from people you don't even follow. And the thing is, sometimes you actually like what you see, right?

○ I like it most of the time.

○ I like it, but not always.

○ I don't like it.

Why do some people like it when information finds them on its own? We're going to unravel this mystery today!

Why Do I Need Information?

The information (content) you absorb turns into your emotions, thoughts, ideas, desires, and perspectives.

It also guides your subsequent decisions.
Often, we purposely search for things that will help us make some sort of choice.

What kind of information helps you make decisions?

I need to decide…

What to gift my friend for their birthday.

Where to continue my education after high school.

So I want to know…

What they dream about, what they like, and what would make them the happiest.

In these examples, everything's very simple: First, you figure out what decision you have to make, and then you intentionally go after the necessary information.

Now imagine if it was flipped: The information finds you on its own and nudges you toward decisions that aren't in your best interest. But they do benefit someone else.

Could this be considered manipulation?

○ Most likely, yes.
○ Not always.
○ I'm not sure what to call it.

"I was browsing online and randomly came across a video where an influencer talked about a cool brand of headphones. I immediately wanted to buy them, even though the ones I have are already good enough."
(Vivienne, 15 years old)

When you figure out what problem you want to solve and what information you need for it, you set a clear **goal** for your search.

To make the right decision, you need to not only find the necessary information but also think through it.

How do you do that? You'll find out in Chapter Two.

Manipulation is when someone tries to influence you and convince you to do what they want, not what you want. One way they do this is by feeding you certain information.

19

The Kitty Experiment

To understand how information finds you, try this experiment (if you use social media).

A recommendation algorithm is an automatic content management system in social media feeds.

Experiment start date: ≤___≥ _____.

Time: _____.

1 Scroll through your feed. Notice which topics pop up the most for you.

Most likely, the algorithm will start showing you more posts similar to those you're liking.

2 Pick a new topic that isn't in your feed. Choose something harmless, like cats, recreational activities, or cooking recipes. For the next week, like posts on this topic regularly.

My topic will be: _____

With each like, you're telling the algorithm, "I like this! I want to see, hear, and read more of this!"

3 Each day, watch to see if more posts related to your new topic start showing up in your feed. After a week, draw a conclusion:

○ They're everywhere!
○ Nothing has changed.

4 Pick a new topic and start liking posts about it. For example, if you were liking posts about cats, now switch to liking posts about dogs. After a while, check to see if your feed changes again.

○ There are fewer posts on the first topic, and more posts on the new topic.
○ Nothing has changed.

Experiment end date: ≤___≥ _____.

Time: _____.

Reflect on the results of the experiment. Keep observing how your social media feed changes and adapts to your activity.

So, Why Is That a Bad Thing?

Many people enjoy automatically getting content they love.

Why?

☐ I don't have to spend time and effort searching.

☐ I don't have to sort and filter information yourself.

☐ I always have an endless stream of my favorite content at my fingertips.

☐ _____

☐ _____

☐ _____

Of course, the information that finds us on its own can be just what we needed in that moment.

"I've always struggled with studying foreign languages. Then I stumbled upon a great video lesson on social media. I followed the creator and started improving my language skills using his lessons." (Denis, 16 years old)

So, it's not a bad thing—if you think carefully about the information, understand how recommendation algorithms work, and know how to control them.

By the way, information doesn't just find you online. In everyday life, we attract information too—sometimes the unwanted kind. For example... rumors and gossip! If someone approves of people sharing this kind of info with them, they'll get more of it. Whether that's good or bad is up to you to decide!

○ Good—Give me all the details!
○ Bad—I don't like talking behind people's backs.
○ I'm indifferent to it.

21

And if, on top of that, you're also not getting enough sleep...

My Informational Diet

Sometimes, we don't feel the negative effects of information right away. Consider this: While you're eating a cheesy slice of pizza, there's nothing else in the world you'd rather be doing. Only later do you start feeling the heaviness in your stomach. And over time, if you eat it regularly, you might start gaining weight without even noticing.

It's the same with information—while you're enjoying content you like, you don't feel tired or burdened by it. Only after some time do you notice that something's not right with your emotions, or realize how much time you've lost.

○ That sounds familiar. ○ That's never happened to me.

To prevent information from having negative effects, it's important to stick to an information diet.

Choose which of these information "eating habits" work for you, and/or come up with your own!

☐ Pay attention to the content that pops up on its own.

☐ Understand how my activity influences recommendation algorithms.

☐ Reflect on how different information affects my emotions and thoughts.

☐ _____

☐ _____

☐ _____

☐ _____

And in the next section, you'll discover the secrets of your attention and learn how to control it, even when you find yourself caught in a whirlwind of information!

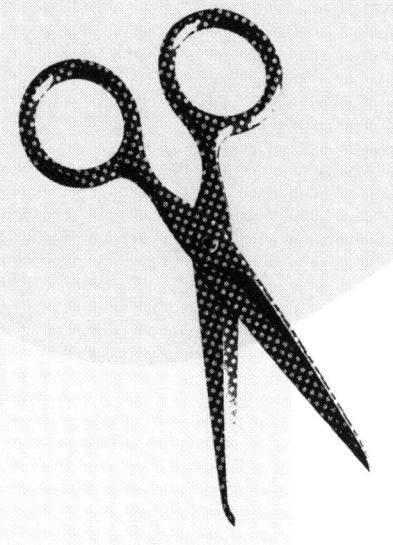

HOW DOES MY ATTENTION WORK?

Attention is a sharp tool, much like a surgeon's scalpel or tailor's scissors. It allows us to cut away the insignificant to focus on what truly matters—to discipline our thinking; to develop concentration and mindfulness. In today's endless stream of information, this is more important than ever. So, let's check if your tool's been sharpened lately.

Let's start with an...

Experiment: Change Your Own Mind

Try this experiment with a friend or family member. You can choose any words and colors. For example, write the word "red" in green and "green" in red.

Quick! Name the color the word is written in as fast as you can. Write down your answers:

BLACK   WHITE

_____   _____

Now, quickly name the size of these words and write it down:

BIG   SMALL

_____   _____

Did you get the color and size of each word right on your first try?
Not everyone can do that!

That's because your brain is used to focusing on the sound of the word, not how it's written. Shifting your focus from one to another can be tough—it takes exercising conscious control over your attention.

And focusing on multiple things at once (like homework and texting) just doesn't work.

Don't believe it? Give your brain another challenge.

What do you see in this picture?

A tree. ○

Animals. ○

Birds. ○

Try focusing on two things at once—like the tree and the animals. It's tough to see both clearly. One will probably pull your attention more and make it hard to concentrate on the other.

Have you ever found it hard to focus on something (like a monotonous paragraph, a complex math problem, or the teacher's droning voice)?

○ All the time.

○ Sometimes.

○ Mostly in school.

○ Never.

How well can you control your attention? Rate yourself on a scale of 0 (I can't focus at all) to 10 (I wield my attention like a surgeon with their scalpel!).

My score:

Turn It On or Turn It Off?

The toughest part is focusing on things that are boring, confusing, or aren't particularly remarkable.

Nobody can stay focused forever, and the great news is you don't have to. It's actually good to let go of control sometimes, allowing yourself to rest and digest everything that's already inside your mind.

When we use willpower to concentrate on what really matters, our **intentional attention** kicks in. That's when our brain gets into focused mode.

When do you think it's okay to turn off **intentional attention** and NOT force yourself to concentrate? And when should it stay turned on?

When I…	Switch on	Switch off
Learn new knowledge and skills.	☐	☐
Want to figure out if a text or video is trustworthy.	☐	☐
Encounter information that doesn't matter to me.	☐	☐
Take a break and just vibe.	☐	☐
Contemplate something important.	☐	☐
Daydream without a specific goal in mind.	☐	☐
Do mental math or think through a question.	☐	☐

Your Inner Butterfly

When intentional attention turns off, **spontaneous attention** takes over. Your brain shifts into diffuse, or, to put it simply, "fluttering" mode.

Spontaneous attention is like a butterfly fluttering from flower to flower, never sticking around for too long. It's light and delicate, always changing its target and quickly moving from one thing to the next.

What usually captures your spontaneous attention when you're doing something important, like reading a textbook or working on an assignment?

- [ ] Notifications on my phone.
- [ ] Vivid memories popping into my head.
- [ ] The smell of food from the kitchen.
- [ ] Random thoughts about things happening in my life.
- [ ] --
- [ ] --

Are there any benefits to spontaneous attention?

Absolutely! It's great for creativity and discovering new things. It also keeps us safe by catching on to unexpected sounds, flashes, strange smells, and other unusual stuff.

Don't be fooled by its apparent lightness and fragility—spontaneous attention can be a serious competitor for intentional attention. It threatens intentional focus by tempting you to get distracted from important but not-so-interesting tasks.

Who Can Capture My Butterfly?

The downside of spontaneous attention? It's easy for **others to control.** They might even set up special traps to catch it.

Has anything ever trapped your attention?

For example:

- ☐ clicking on an internet headline that just caught your eye;
- ☐ mixing up buttons on a website and hitting a bright, flashy ad instead;
- ☐ walking into a store because you saw a big red sale sign;
- ☐ freezing in fear when a sudden scream rings out in a movie;
- ☐ craving a croissant when the smell of fresh baking wafts from a bakery;
- ☐ or _____

Managing "butterfly attention" isn't easy. Sometimes it feels like we have a whole swarm of butterflies in our heads, flying in every direction. We can't focus on anything, like in the first few moments after walking into a giant mall.

This isn't a problem if your goal is just to have fun.

But what if you need to stay alert or focus on something that doesn't attract your butterfly? You've got to awaken your inner hawk!

How to Awaken Your Inner Hawk

When a hawk spots its prey, it locks its gaze onto the target, and nothing can distract it. **Intentional attention** works like a hawk—it has a goal, a clear vision of its path, and the determination to get what it's chasing after.

Surely, there have been times when the hawk inside you lifted its feathered head, and you could focus on something completely. When do you find it easiest to zone in like that?

When:

- ☐ I'm doing something that interests me;
- ☐ I feel rested and full of energy;
- ☐ I find a quiet spot where no one can distract me;
- ☐ _____
- ☐ _____
- ☐ _____

*When you focus on a task for a long time without getting tired, it's called **hyperfocus.***

*On the other hand, when you can't concentrate on anything at all, it's known as **hypofocus** or a **lack of focus.***

Keep an eye on yourself and notice what helps you dial in and hit hyperfocus. If a trick works, make it a **rule** for whenever you need to focus and not get distracted.

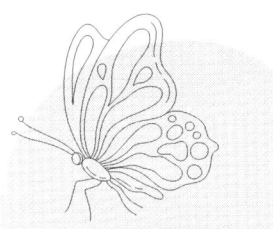

Intentional attention:
Your brain is operating in focus mode.
You're sharp as a hawk.

Spontaneous attention:
Your brain is operating in flutter mode.
You're scattered, like a butterfly.

When you're trying to focus, ask yourself: "Am I acting like a hawk right now, or more like a butterfly?"

Can a butterfly turn into a hawk?

Totally! When spontaneous attention is followed by intentional focus. Imagine your eye catching a stunning book cover. As you start flipping through the tome, you find it interesting and get pulled into the content. The magic here is that while your interest stays, you also gain the willpower to keep your attention fixed on one thing for a long time. Think back—have you ever felt something like this?

How to Measure Attention

The duration—or **span**—of your attention is crucial. It's what lets a hawk circle the sky, scanning for prey all day long. In contrast, spontaneous attention isn't persistent at all—like butterflies that land on something just to lift off in an instant.

You can measure your attention span in minutes—use a clock's second and minute hands to see how long you can keep your gaze on their movement. Or measure it in… liters!

How? Turn the page and give the experiment a shot.

Experiment: Trial by Water

They say you can watch fire and water forever. Is that accurate in your case?

Pour a quarter cup of cold water into a pot and place it on the stove. Concentrate on the water—watch carefully as it changes until it starts to boil.

Did you manage to make it to the end without getting distracted? If so, your attention span is equivalent to about a quarter cup of water! Try adding more water and measure your attention again (it's a good idea to take a short break first to give your mind a rest).

My attention span:

Half a cup.　　One cup.　　Two cups.　　Your own measure.

A true attention guru can do more than wait for the water to boil—they can watch it until it's completely evaporated!

30

Finding it tough to watch the water? Getting distracted?

Try placing a paper boat in the pot and focus on it instead.

What else can you use to measure your attention span? Compete with your family or friends!

Other attention metrics:　　　　　　　　　　　　**My score:**

Number of pages read at once in an interesting book.　　　_____

Number of pages read at once in a boring book.　　　_____

Number of TikToks watched in one go.　　　_____

Number of breaths counted without being sidetracked.　　　_____

Number of game levels completed in one sitting.　　　_____

_____　　　_____

_____　　　_____

_____　　　_____

Keep experimenting and tracking how your attention changes at different times and with different activities. Reflect on whether there's a connection between your attention and the emotions you experience while doing various tasks.

Think about when you get tired faster and why that might be.

What's Interfering With My Attention?

In the water experiment, we saw that attention often shifts to something else. This happens because there are many distractions around and within you.

Observe yourself in different situations and try to pinpoint what usually distracts you. Start by identifying what's currently distracting you from reading this workbook.

Attention can be compared to an antenna catching a specific signal.

When there are too many other signals around, they create informational noise and disrupt the antenna's settings.

External interferences are everything that surrounds you:

- people's voices
- noise from the street
- notifications on your phone
-
-
-
-

Mark the interferences you can always control—by reducing or eliminating them ☒ (for example, by moving to a quiet place or using headphones with neutral background music)—and those that are difficult or impossible to control ⊡.

Internal interferences:

- sensations in your body ☐
- wandering thoughts in your mind ☐
- spontaneous emotions and fantasies ☐
- ☐
- ☐
- ☐

Mark the interferences that are within your control—ones you can reduce or eliminate (for instance, by eating before doing challenging work or mentally setting your fantasies aside for later)—and those that are outside of your realm of influence.

There are two ways to level up your attention, making it as sharp as a hawk's and able to withstand any diversions.

Pick the approach that works for you:
- ○ Learn to eliminate or reduce distractions.
- ○ Learn to focus even among unavoidable distractions.
- ○ I'll take on both of these approaches.

Both paths lead to the same goal—turning attention into your superpower.

So, it makes sense to master both!

Some distractions can even be pleasant—like a message from a friend or a cat curling up right on your desk.

In these cases, veering off course is even more tempting.

How to Make Attention Your Superpower

Attention is the ability to focus not just with your eyes, but also with your ears, nose, fingertips, and maybe even your tongue.

Practice!
　　　　Practice!
　　　　　　　And practice some more!

Here's how:

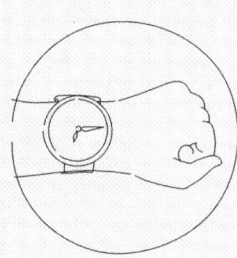

Step 1.

Find time in your schedule

Just a few minutes a day at home or outside. Anywhere you have a moment you can use freely. Experiment in different places—quiet ones without distractions and noisy ones where something might interrupt you.

Step 2.

Choose what you will concentrate on

It can be anything—a spot on the wall, clouds in the sky, your breathing, the texture of a material, a sound, a smell, or the stream of water on your skin during a shower. In different settings and at different times, choose whatever is nearby to focus on.

Step 3.

Decide on the duration of the exercise

Start with a time chunk you can handle... plus a little more. In the beginning, it's okay if that's just one minute. As your exercise your inner hawk more and more, experiment by increasing your focus time.

Step 4.

Try to focus on your chosen object the way a hawk would

Don't set an alarm or timer. Try to feel the length of your focus. This will also help you develop an inner sense of time. Mentally note and name the distractions ("thought," "noise," "notification") that pull you away. After each distraction, bring your attention back to what you're focusing on.

34

Step 5.

Release your focus and assess how concentrated you managed to be

Think about how often your attention lost focus and fluttered away like a butterfly. What distractions got in your way, and how did you manage to bring your focus back?

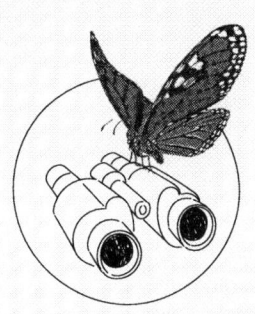

Jot down how many practice sessions you were able to complete in one week:

When your attention starts to waver and you feel the urge to jump to another task, like reaching for your smartphone or heading to the fridge, it's **crucial to recognize that moment**. That's precisely when you can stop yourself and bring your focus back.

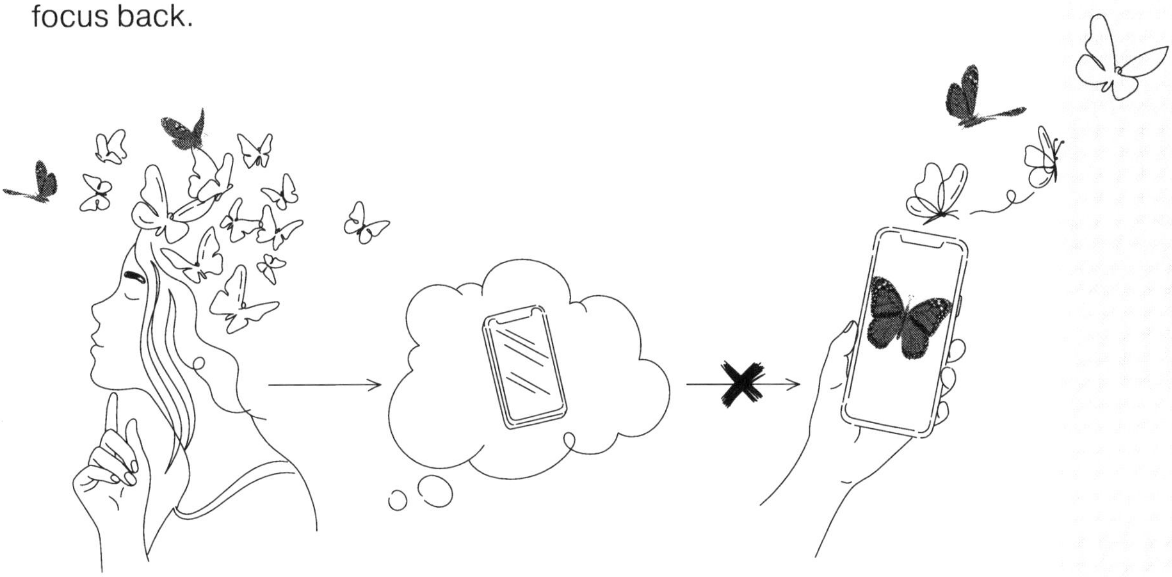

| Attention wanes | You feel the urge to check your phone | You pick up your phone and open Instagram |

Tell yourself, "Stop!"

Contrary to how it might feel, the all-too-familiar sound of a notification doesn't call for immediate action. You can take your time, breathe, and respond with intention.

And if you've managed to harness your inner hawk while reading this chapter, mark the tips and tricks you will start using in your daily life:

- [ ] Asking myself: "Is my attention like a butterfly or a hawk right now?"
- [ ] Mentally activating intentional focus when it matters.
- [ ] Noticing when my butterfly attention has been caught in a trap.
- [ ] Measuring my attention to see how it changes and improves.
- [ ] Identifying distractions and working on controlling them.
- [ ] Recognizing the moment when my focus itches to switch objects.
- [ ] Regularly training my attention.
- [ ] Telling myself "Stop!" when I feel the urge to get distracted at the wrong moment.

Might I be lying to myself?

Is this true or not?

Could my trust be blind?

CAN'T FOOL ME?
Critical thinking tools to understand yourself, others, and discover the truth.

Are there any real arguments here?

How can I fact-check this?

How can I convince others that I'm right?

- Can I trust what I see in this video?
- Am I sure about this?
- What if this is disinformation or a deepfake?
- Is what they're trying to convince me of proven?
- This isn't a thinking trap by any chance?
- Is this site a credible source?
- What information am I lacking?
- Are the things I'm being taught definitely true?
- Is this expert actually knowledgeable or just pretending?

WHAT IS CRITICAL THINKING AND WHY DO YOU NEED IT?

People often say, "Think critically! Be rational! Don't believe everything you hear!" Do those things mean you should:

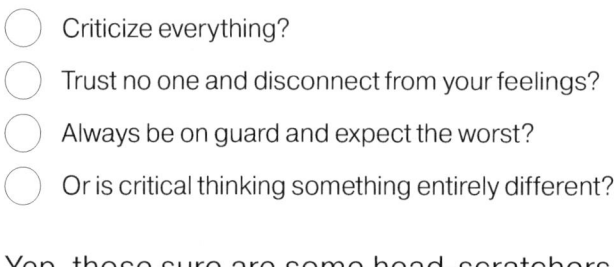

- ◯ Criticize everything?
- ◯ Trust no one and disconnect from your feelings?
- ◯ Always be on guard and expect the worst?
- ◯ Or is critical thinking something entirely different?

Yep, those sure are some head-scratchers. Don't worry, we'll figure the answers out together and understand what critical thinking really means.

Don't mistake critical thinking for having a negative view of the world. They are not the same thing.

Fact or Fiction

Which of these statements do you think are true? Try to answer quickly, with the first thing that comes to mind. Then check to see what's actually accurate. Compare your opinion to what we call facts. A fact is something that has been proven to be true.

	I think that's true	No, I don't think that's the case
The Great Wall of China is visible from space.	☐	☐
Lightning never strikes the same place twice.	☐	☐
Vikings wore helmets with horns in ancient times.	☐	☐
Touching a toad will cause warts to grow on your hand.	☐	☐
A goldfish's memory lasts no more than three seconds.	☐	☐
People use only 10% of their brain.	☐	☐
The elephant is the largest mammal.	☐	☐

What sources did you use to look up this information and verify it? Can you trust these sources?

Being able to check and confirm or disprove your knowledge, beliefs based on personal experience, and conclusions is a key skill in critical thinking.

When and how this skill might come in handy

When...

I'm being bombarded with ads to buy some product.

Someone tries to scare me into believing that touching a toad will give me warts.

The news reports that eating unwashed fruit can make you seriously ill.

Why...

To check if this item is really as fantastic as they make it out to be.

To verify if touching a toad is truly dangerous (because I really, really want to touch it).

To find out what illnesses you can get from eating unwashed fruit and how dangerous those really are.

_____

_____

_____

_____

_____

_____

_____

In the next section, you'll learn more about how to test information against reality.

Corroborating information is useful in a wide range of life situations. Without critical thinking, a person is not only unable to do this, but also fails to understand why it's important.

Keep a Cool Head

Imagine that you're a guest at someone's house. They pour you some tea then proceed to stir it... with a toothbrush. Are you suddenly not thirsty anymore? What if you knew for certain the toothbrush was brand-new—came straight out of the box and has never been used by anyone?

Let's paint more of a picture, shall we?

Guests are served a dish of fried mealworm larvae and juicy spiders, baked to a crispy perfection. ☐ ☐

Apple juice is poured from a pitcher with someone's false teeth floating inside. ☐ ☐

The dessert is composed of chocolate pastries shaped like dog poop. ☐ ☐

If you're feeling courageous, you could run this experiment with your friends to see if they grimace and gag, or if they'd be willing to try your treats.

In some countries, insect-based food is quite popular. We might critique such dishes, but that will have nothing to do with critical thinking, which tells us that insect food is harmless and nutritious— that's a fact.

This might be the party of your dreams—no judgment here—, but for many people, things like these evoke unpleasant emotions (usually disgust). Even when guests know that the poop is fake, the teeth are made of jelly, and the insects are perfectly edible.

Why might the guests at this dinner party refuse to eat, even if they know the treats are safe and completely edible?

☐ People often trust their emotions and feelings more than knowledge and facts.

☐ Strong emotions are clouding their judgment, making it hard to accurately assess what's happening.

☐ These individuals lack critical thinking skills.

☐ Or _____

Keeping a cool head is another critical thinking skill. It means you can reason rationally based on facts rather than letting emotions take the wheel.

Without this skill, decisions would be made purely based on emotions—both pleasant and unpleasant. For instance, the thrill of getting a new smartphone might make you neglect evaluating its features and wave away the question of whether you really need it.

Do you have to be an emotionless robot to engage in critical thinking?

Calculating… calculating… Definitely not. Some emotions and feelings can actually be helpful. **Curiosity** motivates us to seek out new knowledge and discover valuable facts. The **fear** of making a wrong decision encourages a more thorough analysis of information. And **pride** in your knowledge keeps you intellectually sharp, broadens your horizons, and motivates you to share your expertise with others.

Sometimes, emotions make us reluctant to accept certain facts because we're afraid of disappointment or letting go of dreams and beliefs we see as part of our identity.

"Being the kind of person who welcomes the truth, even if it's painful, is what makes other people willing to be honest with you," advises Julia Galef, author of The Scout Mindset.

"I Know That I Know Nothing"

Intellectual laziness is critical thinking's worst enemy.

Speaking of taking pride in your knowledge—this quote is commonly attributed to the ancient Greek philosopher Socrates. But don't take my word for it: Check it out yourself to see if that claim is true and find out how long ago this was said.

○ Yep, Socrates said that.
○ Socrates didn't actually say that.
○ I'm too lazy to check…

The philosopher who said this certainly wasn't a fool, but he also wasn't overly confident in his own correctness. Why do you think that might be?

☐ He understood that it's impossible to know everything in the world.

☐ He recognized that he could be wrong in his judgments.

☐ He acknowledged that his knowledge could become outdated.

☐ Or _____

Being like a 21st-century Socrates means recognizing the limits of your knowledge, having the courage to admit your mistakes, and understanding that the world can change faster than our perceptions of it. This is another critical thinking skill known as **intellectual humility.**

To accept the imperfection of your knowledge and beliefs while continuing to explore the world means thinking and living like a philosopher and a scholar.

Have you ever genuinely admitted that someone else was right and you had made a mistake?

○ I can't think of an instance.
○ I have, but it was a challenge for me.
○ Yes, it's easy for me to admit when I'm wrong.

The ability to internally acknowledge your mistakes and gaps in knowledge is an imperative skill for a critical thinker. Furthermore, admitting your errors to others is an act deserving of respect.

Check how confident you are in your knowledge:

Rate it on a scale from zero, which means "I have no confidence that I know the answer," to 100, which means "I am absolutely certain that I know the answer." Assess any of your knowledge and beliefs about the world, yourself, and others.

2 + 2 = 4?	0 10 20 30 40 50 60 70 80 90 **(100)**
Does the Sun orbit the Earth?	0 10 20 30 40 50 60 70 80 90 100
How do energy drinks affect your health?	0 10 20 30 40 50 60 70 80 90 100
How does my friend really feel about me?	0 10 20 30 40 50 60 70 80 90 100
_ _ _ _ _ _ _ _ _ _ _ _ _ _ _ _ _ _ _	0 10 20 30 40 50 60 70 80 90 100
_ _ _ _ _ _ _ _ _ _ _ _ _ _ _ _ _ _ _	0 10 20 30 40 50 60 70 80 90 100
_ _ _ _ _ _ _ _ _ _ _ _ _ _ _ _ _ _ _	0 10 20 30 40 50 60 70 80 90 100
_ _ _ _ _ _ _ _ _ _ _ _ _ _ _ _ _ _ _	0 10 20 30 40 50 60 70 80 90 100

This isn't a test where you need to score top marks. Doubting your knowledge is perfectly fine—it actually keeps your mind open. Plus, doubts point out what information you're missing and what areas to grow in.

Not knowing something, reconsidering the correctness of your beliefs and ideas, and openly admitting you're wrong is nothing to be ashamed of.

"Discovering you were wrong is an update, not a failure, and your worldview is a living document meant to be revised." — Julia Galef

Black and White Thinking

Imagine if the whole world suddenly turned black and white. No more considering the complexities of life—just automatically choosing between two options, opinions, or decisions. For example:

I agree with this

I'm either a straight-A student **or** I don't try at all in any of my classes. ☐

My peers are either my friends **or** my enemies. ☐

I must look perfect **or** not even bother leaving the house. ☐

I have to lead a totally healthy lifestyle, **or** there's no point in exercising once a week. ☐

Everyone falls into one of two categories: selfish **or** selfless. ☐

It might seem like this approach simplifies life, but that's a delusion. The real world is bursting with colors and shades. Between any extremes, there are countless options.

Try looking at each statement more broadly, adding in as many "hues" as possible. You'll discover how many alternatives there are that we might not always consider.

For example:

- I get straight A's in all subjects.
- I get straight A's in select subjects.
- I get good grades in all subjects.
- I get good grades in select subjects.
- I try to do well in all subjects.
- I try to do well in select subjects.
- I try to do well in just one subject.
- I don't try to do well in any subject.

---

*When we reduce any choice to just two options, it's called a **false dilemma**.*

*The ability to see a range of options in any question is called **intellectual flexibility**. This helps your thinking become both broader and more precise.*

Breadth, Depth, and Precision

If critical thinking were a gadget, which one would it be?

○ A microscope.
○ A telescope.
○ A magnifying glass.
○ A ruler.
○ A kaleidoscope.
○ Or _

It's hard to imagine critical thinking as just one tool or device. After all, it helps us expand the boundaries of our usual perspectives and look at the world more **broadly**, viewing things from completely different angles and turning our assumptions upside down. It digs **deeper** even where everything seems obvious. It analyzes information with the highest possible **precision**, noticing the tiniest details and hidden elements. It also helps us piece together a coherent worldview from disparate facts, like assembling a mosaic, and prompts us to regularly measure the completeness and accuracy of our knowledge.

That is, of course, if we remember to press all these critical thinking buttons in our heads. But is that always necessary?

THINK BROADLY AND DEEPLY

When Critical Thinking Is (Un)Necessary

Just like intentional attention, critical thinking—as useful as it is—can **drain our intellectual energy**. That's why it's important to know how to not only turn it on but also turn it off.

One of the aspects of critical thinking is **intentional ("hawk-like") attention**. Critical thinking won't be of much help to us if we can't focus on the information we're trying to evaluate to begin with.

But we don't need to view the world through the prism of critical thinking at every moment of our lives. Try to decide for yourself when to turn it on and when it's not needed.

Critical Thinking: On	Critical Thinking: Off
When listening to a lecture	*When making art and being creative*
When reading political news	*When watching a sci-fi series*

You decide when to turn on your critical thinking. No one can force you to do it. And how to harness the power of critical thinking to see the world as it truly is—that's what the next pages are all about.

Let's Summarize What We Learned

Critical thinking is the ability to:

	X	√
Test your beliefs, knowledge, and convictions.	☐	☐
Question what you know.	☐	☐
Recognize the limits of your knowledge and strive to expand them.	☐	☐
Make decisions with a clear, rational mind.	☐	☐
Keep your mind open to new information.	☐	☐
Move beyond a black-and-white view of the world.	☐	☐
Think broadly, deeply, and precisely.	☐	☐
Criticize and mock everything all the time.	☐	☐
Believe in nothing and no one.	☐	☐
Completely abandon your emotions and feelings.	☐	☐
Think critically every single minute of your life.	☐	☐

TELL YOURSELF "STOP"
How to Verify Information and Not Be Deceived

It's all over the news: Sharks are attacking tourists in the Red Sea. Social media feeds are flooded with posts about yet another apocalypse. Acquaintances boast about their romance movie-worthy conquests. Meanwhile, teachers keep lecturing you (no pun intended) about smartphones ruining your eyesight and lowering your intelligence. How are you supposed to know what to believe?

Liar, Liar, Pants on Fire

People are constantly sharing information with each other. Some of it is true, while other information only seems true. Sometimes people deceive one another and **intentionally spread disinformation**, others only **accidentally misinform**. Is it always considered lying when you don't tell the truth?

In the news article titled "Bloodthirsty Killer Sharks Terrorize Tourists," it's reported that sharks regularly attack vacationers on the beaches of the Red Sea. The authors know that such attacks are rare—there are between five and 10 incidents per year, mostly affecting those who swim in the open sea or in restricted areas. However, they intentionally exaggerate, prioritizing getting clicks, likes, and comments over the truth.

○ That's a lie and misinformation!

○ That's misinformation, but not necessarily a lie.

Sidebar:

Information that does not match reality is called **misinformation** or a **fake**. But it's not always a lie.

Headlines written in a way that makes your eyes widen and your hands jerk to click on them are called **clickbait**. They usually distort and overstate real events.

An influencer claims that people's abilities and character depend on their race, nationality, and gender. You know that scientific research says otherwise. However, the blogger genuinely believes in what they are saying.

◯ That's a lie and misinformation!
◯ That's misinformation, but not necessarily a lie.

Deshawn is trying to convince a classmate to buy his phone. He knows that its touch screen is faulty and everything takes forever to load, which is why he wants to exchange it. But he tells his classmate, "Man, I'm so bummed about giving up this phone—it works so well! But I have to sell it because I got a new one as a gift."

◯ That's a lie and misinformation!
◯ That's misinformation, but not necessarily a lie.

Strictly speaking, a lie, or disinformation, is when a person knows for certain that what they are saying or writing is false, and intentionally exaggerates or downplays the truth. On the other hand, if someone shares false information but genuinely believes it to be true, that can hardly be considered a lie. This is misinformation, and is more like a **misconception** or **self-deception**.

Misconceptions and Self-Deception

Each of us can have misconceptions. With their help, we deceive our own selves without even realizing it. Critical thinking weeds these misconceptions from our mind.

"I used to think flying was way more dangerous than taking a bus or train. Every time a plane crashed, it was all over the news, and that really freaked me out. But then I found out that planes are actually safer than other types of transport. Latest stats say there's only about one accident for every 830,000 flights!" (Dustin, 15 years old)

◯ I checked! Dustin's information is correct.

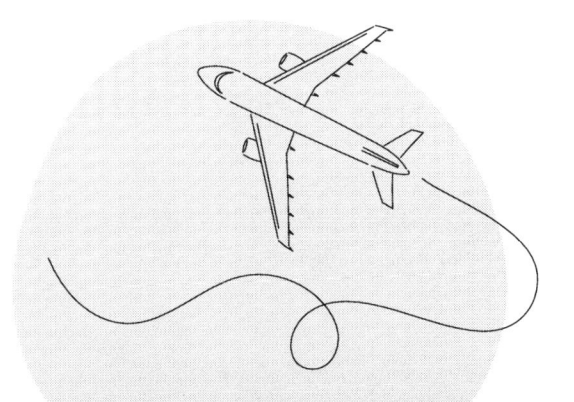

When someone makes judgments about people's personal qualities based on their race, nationality, gender, or age, it's called a **stereotype**.

When such statements are negative, they're known as **prejudice**.

Misconceptions, stereotypes, and prejudices are like funhouse mirrors (without the fun) that distort everything you try to get a good look at.

51

What misconceptions have you had in the past?

Write down a few misconceptions that you've managed to recognize and change.

We can be mistaken not only about events and phenomena in the world but also about ourselves—such as misjudging our own abilities or health.

Reflecting on our old misconceptions helps us see that not everything we know or believe is right. It also shows how our thinking evolves and gets clearer over time.

STOP! Give Me the Facts!

If you're doubting whether a piece of information is true, use the critical thinking acronym STOP. It involves four simple steps:

S—Scan the information.

T—Try out different roles.

O—On the prowl for facts.

P—Prove they're really facts.

The STOP method works with news articles and other publications where people describe real events, share their opinions, offer advice, and make recommendations.

Let's put it to the test! Right now, open any article, post, or section of a book—any text that catches your interest.

S—Scan the information

Scan the text and illustrations to form an initial impression. Pay attention to the following:

	More like the first	More like the second
Is the information presented in a detached (unemotional) manner, or is it overly emotional (e.g., funny, frightening, angering)?	+1	−1
Does the text have good grammar, or are there obvious mistakes, typos, and awkward sentences that stand out?	+1	−1
Is the text attributed to a certain author, or is it unclear who wrote it?	+1	−1
Does the author reference other sources (books, articles, videos, interviews) or provide data without citing the source?	+1	−1

Often, we stop at the scanning stage. If the information doesn't immediately cause us to resist or doubt it, we're perfectly happy believing it without further questions. But that's usually not enough.

The higher the total score, the more trustworthy the text. If the total score is negative, it makes sense to be skeptical of the information, meaning to doubt its reliability.

T—Try out different roles

You can look at information from different perspectives. When you try out a new role or viewpoint, you often see things in fresh, unexpected ways. Try examining the information from various angles:

- **A lazy reader** doesn't want to think too hard—what kind of impression would they get? Don't trust that impression!

- **A conscientious scientist** who only trusts what has been proven—would you have enough evidence if you were in their shoes? Do you still have questions after reading or watching this content, which the information didn't cover?

- **The creator of this content** (influencer, journalist, commentator)—what personal goals might they have? Do their goals align with yours? Is the author trying to influence you or encourage you to take certain actions?

Switching between different roles and perspectives is a sure-fire way to avoid **tunnel vision**—the tendency to see something from one limited, fixed angle.

O—On the prowl for facts

Now is the moment to switch on your inner hawk, to be sharp-sighted as you go on the prowl... for facts.

Facts are events and phenomena that actually occurred, objects that exist in reality, or proven connections between events, objects, and phenomena.

For example, there are facts about your appearance. Eye color, height, and weight are measurable and verifiable facts. There might be a relationship between your height and weight—this too can be measured and confirmed.

However, your attractiveness is not a fact. When people say someone is attractive or unattractive, it's a **personal opinion**, not a fact. Unlike eye color, height, weight, and other specific physical parameters, attractiveness as a general trait can't be measured.

The process of verifying facts is called **fact-checking**. There are professionals whose jobs largely consist of this—journalists and researchers.

Take another diligent look at the materials you're analyzing. Identify and list everything that can be considered facts.

_____

_____

_____

_____

_____

_____

_____

More facts typically means higher credibility. But be careful! Just because something is presented as a fact doesn't mean it actually is one.

54

P—Prove they're really facts

It looks like a fact, it sounds like a fact, but really it's just a... factoid! A **factoid** is presented as a fact but isn't backed up by any evidence.

A fact can become a factoid if someone exaggerates it, adds fabricated details, or, conversely, hides important information.

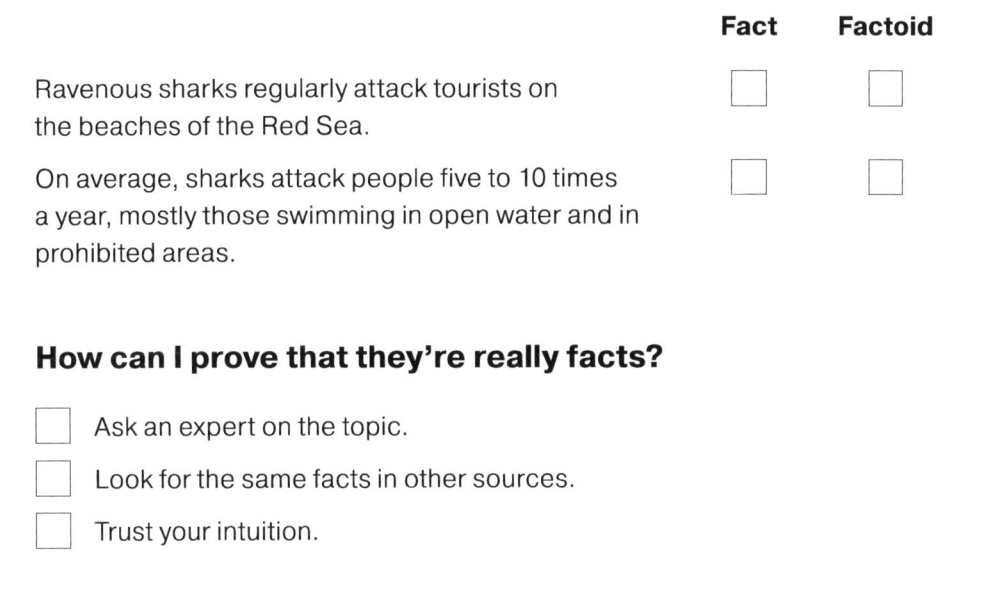

	Fact	Factoid
Ravenous sharks regularly attack tourists on the beaches of the Red Sea.	☐	☐
On average, sharks attack people five to 10 times a year, mostly those swimming in open water and in prohibited areas.	☐	☐

How can I prove that they're really facts?

☐ Ask an expert on the topic.
☐ Look for the same facts in other sources.
☐ Trust your intuition.

If you know someone who's knowledgeable about the topic, you can ask them to evaluate the facts. In the next section, we'll discuss how to determine which experts are worth trusting.

Looking for confirmation of facts in other sources is a good way to verify them. If multiple sources provide the same facts, the likelihood that they are accurate increases.

Intuition, however, is unlikely to help you verify facts. Sometimes, what intuitively seems like obvious truth turns out to be fiction. And conversely, real facts can appear so incredible that we can't even believe them in our imagination.

Intuition and imagination are great tools for creative thinking, but they can hinder critical thinking.

Check each fact you've noted to ensure it's not a factoid.

When a hawk scans the ground from the sky, they can easily distinguish a rabbit from a rabbit-shaped rock. Likewise, by being sharp as hawks, we can distinguish true facts from factoids.

You'll learn about which sources you can trust in the upcoming sections.

Now, make your final decision on how much you can trust the information you're analyzing.

◯ I can trust it because:

_____
_____
_____
_____
_____
_____

Or

◯ I can only trust it partially because:

_____
_____
_____
_____
_____
_____

Or

◯ I can't trust it at all because:

_____
_____
_____
_____
_____
_____
_____

You can start trusting information without thorough analysis, but that trust is blind. **Rational trust**, on the other hand, is built on the conclusions drawn from analysis. In this case, you can always explain to yourself and others why you chose to trust or not trust the information.

Mind In a Whirl?

Disinformation, lies, self-deception, misconceptions, stereotypes, prejudices, facts, factoids—are all these terms making your head spin? Don't worry and don't rush; give yourself time to digest it all.

And we'll help you review!

Got it!

People say or write things that aren't true and aren't backed up by evidence. This is **misinformation**. ☐

When people knowingly say or write something false and do it intentionally, it's **disinformation**, **deception**, and **lies**. ☐

We may believe information that isn't true. This is **self-deception** or a **misconception**. ☐

When someone expresses an opinion about people's abilities and qualities based on their race, nationality, gender, or age, that's a **stereotype**. ☐

A negative opinion about the abilities and qualities of people based on their race, nationality, gender, or age is called a **prejudice**. ☐

Something really happens that can be measured, verified, confirmed, and proven. That's a **fact**. ☐

Something that looks like a fact but isn't actually backed up by evidence is called a **factoid**. ☐

TRUST, BUT VERIFY!
Sources Under the Lens of Critical Thinking

Great news! You get an email with confetti graphics all over it, claiming that you had been entered into a lottery randomly drawn from a million users. And you're one of the lucky winners! To claim your large prize, you just need to provide the organizers with your passport details.

What would you do?

◯ Reply ASAP with a photo of my passport!

◯ Delete the email or mark it as spam.

◯ Or _____

This hypothetical situation (or maybe not so hypothetical) brings up a key question for critical thinking—how can we verify a source to determine if it's trustworthy?

My Information Sources

We get all kinds of information—news, quotes, educational materials, advice, recommendations, and even memes—from a variety of sources. What sources do you use most often? And which ones do you consider the most reliable?

	How often I use it	How reliable it is
Books and textbooks	▨▨☐☐☐	▨▨▨☐☐
Articles on websites	☐☐☐☐☐	☐☐☐☐☐
Social media posts	☐☐☐☐☐	☐☐☐☐☐
YouTube videos	☐☐☐☐☐	☐☐☐☐☐
TikToks	☐☐☐☐☐	☐☐☐☐☐
Email newsletters	☐☐☐☐☐	☐☐☐☐☐
TV news broadcasts	☐☐☐☐☐	☐☐☐☐☐
Print magazines and newspapers	☐☐☐☐☐	☐☐☐☐☐
_____	☐☐☐☐☐	☐☐☐☐☐
_____	☐☐☐☐☐	☐☐☐☐☐
_____	☐☐☐☐☐	☐☐☐☐☐
_____	☐☐☐☐☐	☐☐☐☐☐

Do you use artificial intelligence as a source of information?

Visually compare how often you use each source with how reliable they are. Are the sources you use most often the most reliable ones?

What Is Source Reliability?

Here's what some of your peers said:

○ *"Reliable sources are ones that my friends recommend, like videos on social media." (Aidan, 14)*

○ *"I think a source is reliable if I know it well. For example, my favorite magazine or blog." (Shreya, 15)*

○ *"I trust the most popular sources. I mean, if they weren't reliable, why would people use them?" (Owen, 14)*

○ *"I feel like, in the modern day, there aren't any reliable, truthful sources left. So I don't trust anything!" (Kotomi, 15)*

Who do you agree with?
Mark with a
V

And who do you disagree with?
Mark with a
X

Once you've finished reading this section, come back to this page and see if your opinion has changed.

Hold Up, What Even Is Reliability?

Just like with information, the reliability of a source means we can trust it. But for that trust to be rational, we need some solid reasons. Can a source's popularity or recommendations from friends be enough?

Choose one of the sources you use for studying.

Then, see if it holds up using this **reliability test:**

How do you check reliability if the source is an AI chat? Do you ever think about that when interacting with AI?

	If so…
The source of information is not anonymous; you know exactly who the author or authors are.	+1
The source is recommended by experts (such as teachers, professors, science journalists, or specialists in the field).	+1
The source is backed not just by the author or authors, but also by an organization (like a university, online school, tech company, or well-known media outlet).	+1
The source (such as a book, article, video, or documentary) has been highly praised by a renowned expert (like a well-known scientist or entrepreneur).	+1
The source includes publication dates, and the materials are generally no older than 10 years (for rapidly changing topics like "AI Technology," no older than a year).	+1
The source is free from obvious errors, typos, and disclaimers; the information is well-organized and professionally presented.	+1
The material includes references to other sources, including research and academic papers.	+1

The higher the score, the more likely the source can be considered reliable. Can any single source be 100% trustworthy? Probably not. But if multiple sources provide consistent information, you can be more confident in both the content and where it's coming from.

Why the Quality of a Source Matters

Think of the flow of information like a flow of water. It could be a clear mountain stream. Or a jet from a beautiful decorative fountain. It might be a trickle from a downspout. Or a gush from a burst sewage pipe.

A mountain crevice, a fountain, a downspout, or a sewage pipe—these are all sources. Would you rather consume sewer water or spring water? I bet I know your answer.

The same goes for information sources—their quality impacts the quality of the information we get from them.

Try to match each image with specific examples of sources you've come across. You can also invent your own images.

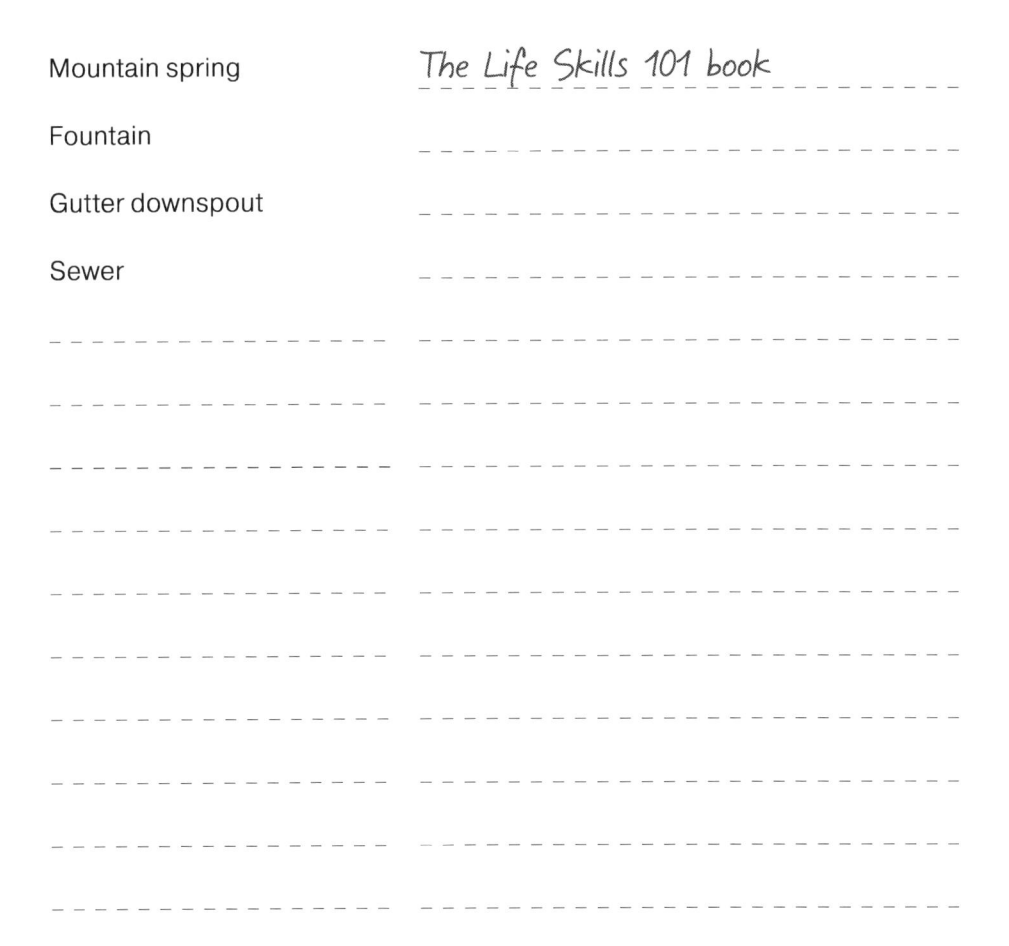

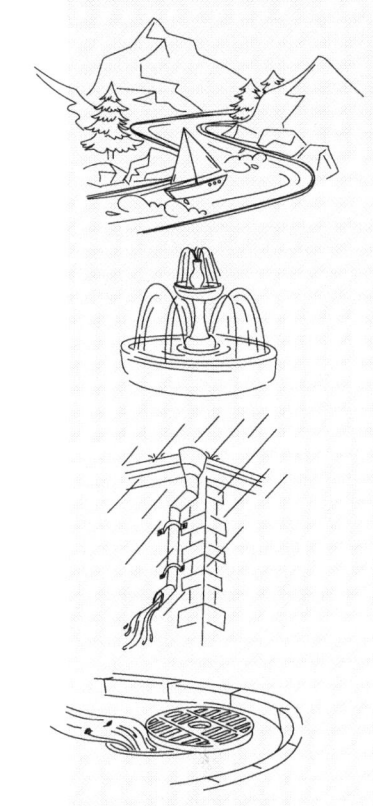

Mountain spring — *The Life Skills 101 book*

Fountain — _____

Gutter downspout — _____

Sewer — _____

_____

_____

_____

_____

_____

_____

_____

_____

_____

_____

Would you want to drink from an untested source, like an unexplored body of water? Dirty water is harmful to your health. And can information be harmful to your mental health or thinking?

In your opinion, what might a letter from an unknown sender promising a big win resemble?

Two-Tiered Trustworthiness

If a source is reliable, does that mean everything it says is beyond doubt?

◯ Yes, always.   ◯ No, not always.   ◯ I have to think about it.

On one hand, a good source usually means good info. On the other hand, even reservoirs can become contaminated—meaning even reliable sources can misinform sometimes. So if the information is important and could impact you, it's wise to double-check both the source and the content.

A RELIABLE SOURCE + RELIABLE INFORMATION = TRUST

The reliability test   The STOP method (see page 52).

Sometimes, even a shady source can have accurate information. But trusting it can be tough if the source itself is questionable. It's like the philosophical fable "The Boy Who Cried Wolf."

A young shepherd was watching his flock of sheep when he grew bored and decided to cry out, "Wolf! Help! There's a wolf!" The villagers rushed to his aid, only to find that there was no wolf. The next day, he did the same thing, and again, no wolf. On the third day, when a wolf actually appeared and the boy called for help, the villagers did not believe him and no one came to help him save the sheep.

Have you ever lost trust in a source that misled you a few times?

Modern generative AI technologies can create photos and videos that are indistinguishable from real ones. Can we still trust something just because it's supposedly documented with a photo or video?

Not Every Source Needs to Be Checked

If you were to scrutinize every single source, you'd have no time left for anything else.

And let's be honest, sometimes we're tempted to peek into a downspout or dive into a sewer just out of curiosity.

Try to figure out when it's worth double-checking a source and when it's not really necessary.

When I want to:

Study for exams. ☐

Learn about how to stay healthy. ☐

Watch funny videos. ☐

Find side hustle opportunities. ☐

Choose a diet or workout plan. ☐

Scroll through memes. ☐

Get advice on investing. ☐

Knowing the general principles of checking information and its sources will save you time in the long run. Thanks to these exercises kicking your critical thinking into gear, you'll get faster and faster at determining what to trust and what to question.

Rumor has it you shouldn't trust gossip

A river starts at a pure mountain spring. But as it flows, it gathers dirt and trash. The same goes for rumors. Even if they start out being true, they often get distorted and "polluted" along the way. So, no matter what feelings a certain rumor stirs up in you, trusting them is like diving head-first into a sewer. Sadly, some people actually enjoy wallowing in the muck.

Before sharing anything with others, consider this: Are you contributing to the spread of misinformation?

Breaking News!

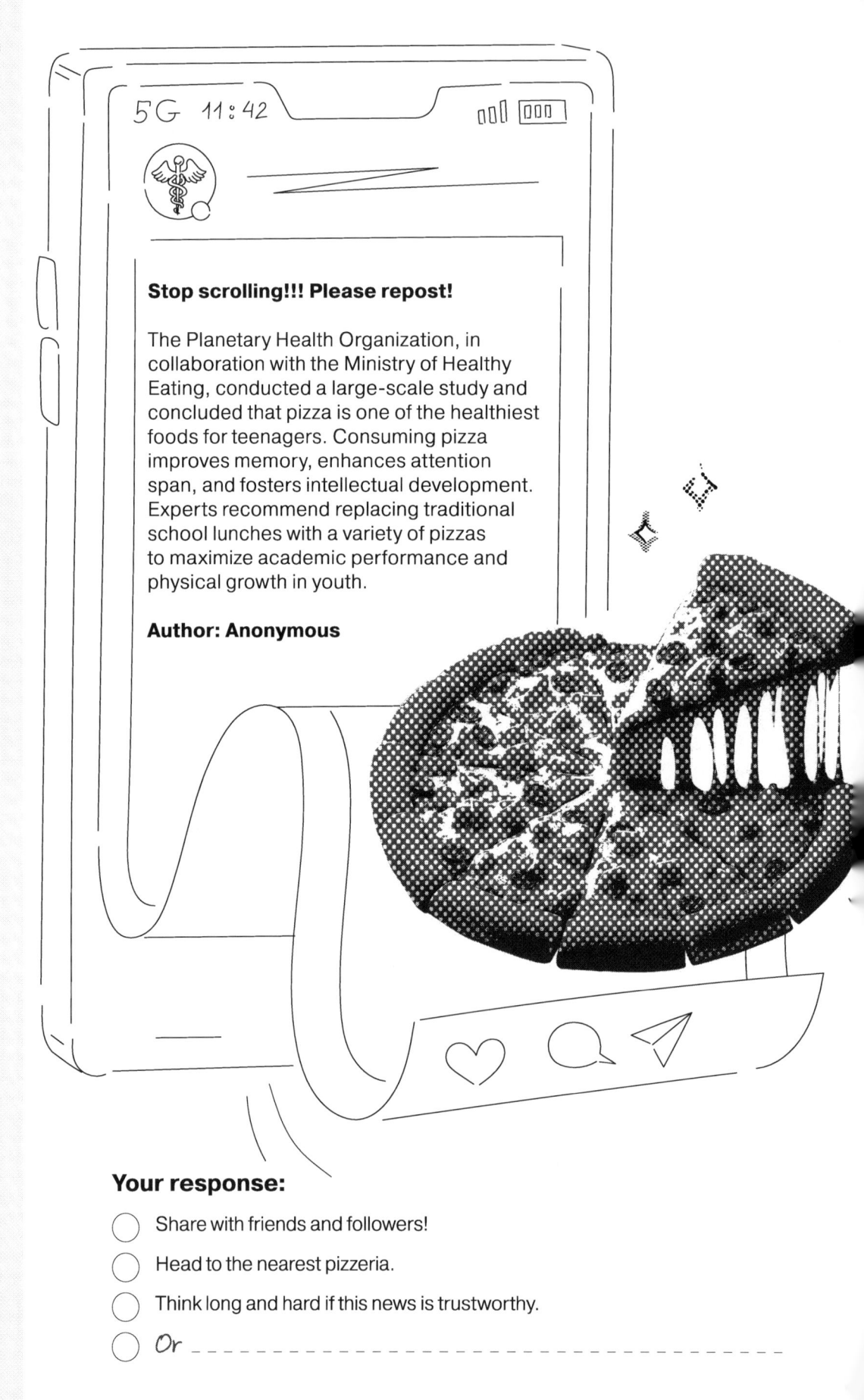

Stop scrolling!!! Please repost!

The Planetary Health Organization, in collaboration with the Ministry of Healthy Eating, conducted a large-scale study and concluded that pizza is one of the healthiest foods for teenagers. Consuming pizza improves memory, enhances attention span, and fosters intellectual development. Experts recommend replacing traditional school lunches with a variety of pizzas to maximize academic performance and physical growth in youth.

Author: Anonymous

Can another person be a source of information? Find out more on the following pages.

Your response:

◯ Share with friends and followers!

◯ Head to the nearest pizzeria.

◯ Think long and hard if this news is trustworthy.

◯ Or _____

64

To make choosing the right option a bit easier, let's review:

- [ ] We get information from all sorts of sources.
- [ ] Sources can be reliable or unreliable.
- [ ] A reliable source is one that doesn't mislead you.
- [ ] To assess a source's reliability, you need to put it to the test.
- [ ] Even reliable sources can have inaccurate information.
- [ ] That's why reliable sources should also be examined under the lens of critical thinking.
- [ ] The quality of the source impacts the quality of the information.
- [ ] Ask yourself: "Am I getting this information from a clean river or a sewer?"

SHOULD YOU ALWAYS LISTEN TO THE EXPERTS?

Trust is the "currency" we pay for reliable, valuable, and helpful information; it's frustrating when we're duped with unimportant details, informational junk food, or outright disinformation. What's even worse is when that trust leads to wasted time, money, or negative impacts on our well-being.

The Cost of a Mistake

Imagine you're in the mood to binge-watch a new series. With so many new releases, it can be hard to choose. So, you decide to look up reviews from popular influencers who cover movies and TV shows.

User film_pop_corn

"This series is the bomb! Every episode has me on the edge of my seat. The characters are so cool. I can't stop watching it! I've just started, but I'm sure the ending will be epic. You absolutely have to check it out—just trust me!"

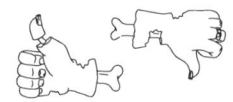

User tv_soul

"This show stuns with its complex plot and well-developed characters. The creators really paid attention to the details, which is evident both in the dialogue and the visuals. The series has been highly praised by critics for the acting and direction. After watching all the seasons, I can confidently say that this is one of the best shows of the year."

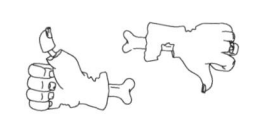

Which review grabs you emotionally? Which one includes not just personal opinions but also factual information?

If you make a mistake choosing a TV show based on a blogger's advice, the worst that might happen is wasting some time. But what if you're choosing a new smartphone, a workout program, a diet plan, or an effective skincare product? What's the cost of a mistake if you confide in a phony expert?

> Emotional statements often capture our attention more than dry facts. But which is more reliable?

What Defines an Expert

An expert is someone who has a deep understanding of a particular topic or field and can share their knowledge with others. Who do you consider to be experts?

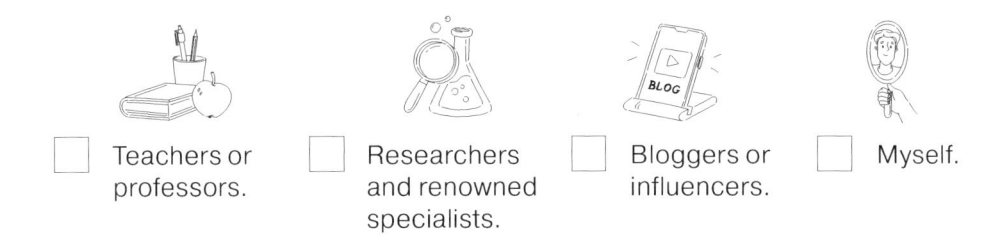

- ☐ Teachers or professors.
- ☐ Researchers and renowned specialists.
- ☐ Bloggers or influencers.
- ☐ Myself.

You can be an expert for someone who knows less than you in a particular area. And for you, an expert can be anyone who knows more about a specific topic.

Do you consider your parents experts? In what topics or issues do you trust their experience and opinions?

What Is an Expert Opinion?

An expert will have an opinion on a range of topics or issues, such as a TV show or sports training. But, big deal. Everyone has opinions. What makes an expert's opinion different?

	Expert	~~Expert~~
"I'm convinced that running is the best thing you can do for your health. Every morning I start with a run, and it gives me energy for the whole day. Give it a try—you won't regret it. Plus, if it comes to that, you'll be able to outrun zombies!"	☐	☐
"Scientific research confirms that regular running improves cardiovascular health, increases endorphin levels, and helps combat depression. This indicates that running is well-researched and its value for maintaining health is proven. For those interested, references to the studies are provided at the end of this post. Therefore, I believe that running can be an excellent exercise and recommend incorporating it into your regular physical activity."	☐	☐

Note that expert statements typically include facts and well-supported conclusions that back up and strengthen their opinions.

FACT ⟶ CONCLUSION ⟶ OPINION (EVALUATION, ADVICE)

People often tend to trust experts whose opinions align with their own views and preferences.

But what matters more? Whether the expert's opinion matches our own beliefs, or whether it's well-supported and logical, even if it challenges our usual way of thinking?

What in the expert's statement about running is based on facts?

Regular running improves cardiovascular health and

What in the expert's statement is the conclusion?

This indicates that running is well-researched

And what is the opinion the expert expresses in their statement?

Therefore, I recommend

Here's a question for you: When someone claims to be an expert but isn't, what is usually sparse or altogether missing from their statements?

○ Facts.   ○ Conclusions.   ○ Opinions.

Statements from pseudo-experts are often extremely opinionated, chock-full of advice and evaluations… but the evidence to support those opinions is nowhere to be found. Their conclusions might sound convincing, but they're based on anecdotal stories and emotions rather than facts.

A pseudo-expert is someone who pretends to be an expert or considers themselves one, but doesn't have sufficient knowledge and experience for the job.

68

From Head to Toe

Finding an expert is only half the battle. You also need to make sure they're actually trustworthy. So, let's put on our critical thinking caps and inspect that expert from head to toe!

Is it possible to be an expert in everything under the sun? Or should a good expert focus on mastering just a few key areas?

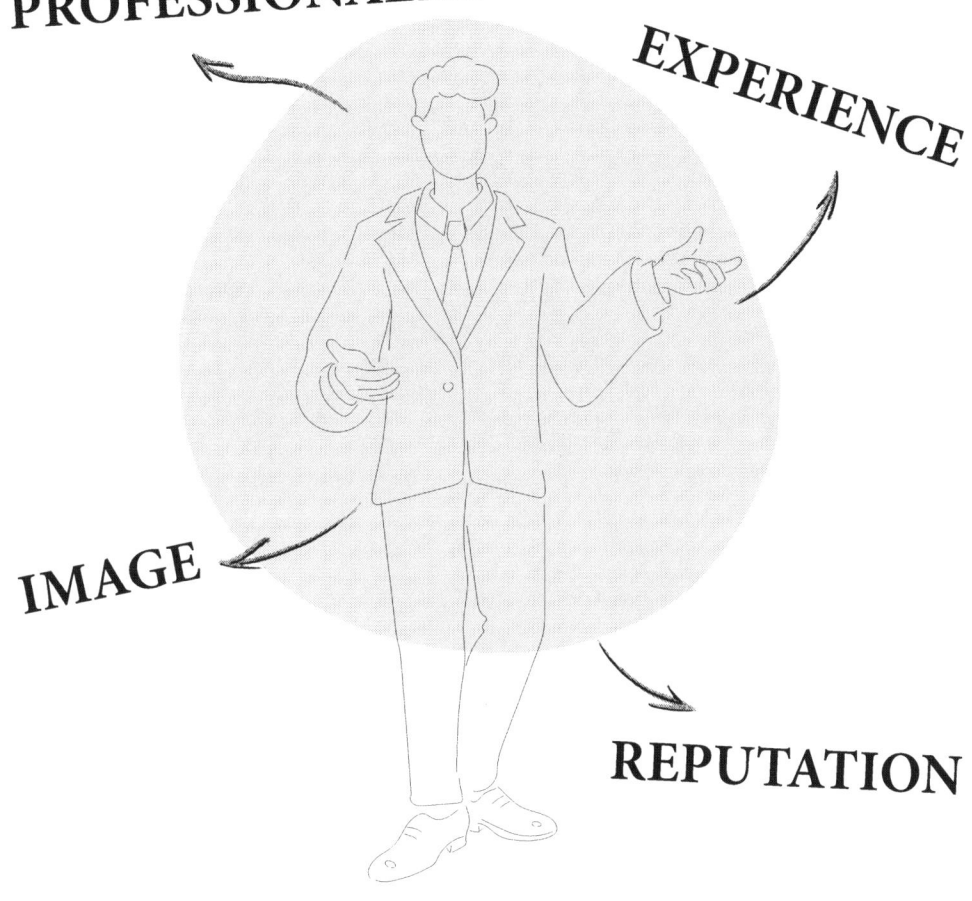

PROFESSIONALISM

EXPERIENCE

IMAGE

REPUTATION

The head—an expert's professionalism.

You probably can't take a literal peek inside the expert's head, but you can definitely assess what's in there by looking at their professionalism, which is a blend of their knowledge and skills.

An expert's education can be just as important. A reputable diploma shows that the expert has formally studied their field. However, if your personal experience of dozing off in the middle of class is any indicator, it doesn't necessarily tell you how much they actually learned.

Would you put your health in the hands of a doctor without a medical degree? What makes following the advice of a wellness blogger without formal education any different?

Sometimes even good experts may disagree. In these cases, none of their opinions should be taken as the absolute truth.

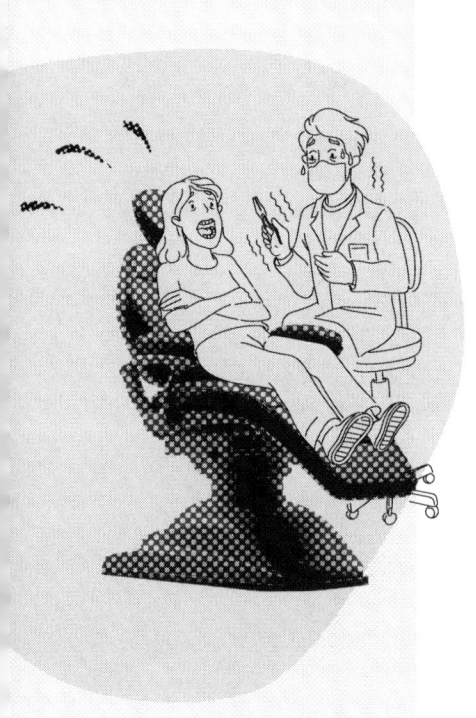

How to evaluate an expert's knowledge

○ A good expert is always completely confident in their knowledge.

or

○ A good expert's opinions align with other experts' opinions.

A good and responsible expert is more like the philosopher Socrates—they recognize that they can't know everything and can't be certain even about what they do know. In contrast, an ignorant person is often the most overconfident.

But if an expert's opinion aligns with the views of other experts on a particular issue, it makes it more likely that they know what they're doing.

The hands—an expert's practical experience.

Not every expert has extensive experience under their belt, and sometimes that's not even necessary. For instance, an expert on Martian soil doesn't need to grow a garden on Mars to understand the subject. However, you probably wouldn't want to be a heart surgeon's first patient. A less frightening example is how a language tutor should have some real-world interaction with native speakers.

Hands-on experience is crucial when an expert's professionalism isn't just about knowledge, but also includes specific practical skills.

The legs—an expert's reputation.

A person's reputation is built on the opinions, evaluations, and reviews from others. It reflects where others stand on the topic of the expert, meaning how well the expert is regarded in your community.

Do you think the number of likes and followers provides meaningful insight into an expert's reputation? Or should these metrics be taken with a grain of salt?

Write down your thoughts to reflect on them further.

Likes often reflect the public's impression of a person. Under the influence of emotions, people don't always accurately assess the competence of their idols.

The suit—an expert's image.

Image is not the same as reputation. It's how an expert presents themselves, how they describe and portray themselves, and the style of communication they use with the public if they're a well-known figure. An image can be deceptive. Behind the mask of a confident and successful expert might be someone who is incompetent or even a fraud.

Whose image do you trust more when you watch videos of experts giving advice on taking care of your health?

Try this experiment with your friends or family: Show them photos of two people who resemble the ones in drawings, and ask which one they would trust more as a health expert.

The results might surprise you! People often fall victim to the **halo effect,** placing too much importance on someone's appearance and behavior when evaluating their competence.

Consider how scammers can manipulate the impression they make on people by altering their image and appearance. And chew on what could happen if you judge an expert solely by their image without knowing anything else about them.

The halo effect occurs when our positive impression of someone in one area causes us to think highly of them in other areas, even if we have no real basis for doing so. For instance, you might be more likely to trust a conventionally attractive influencer on which study routine is best.

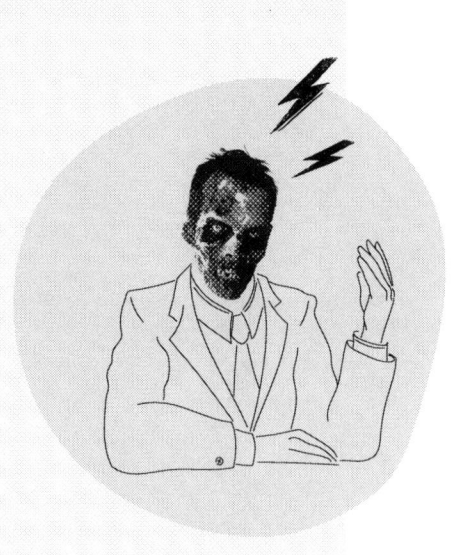

When someone convincing you of something monologues for hours, shoehorning in obscure terms consisting of countless syllables wherever they can, you might mistake that for expertise. What it really is is **obfuscation**, or intentionally complicating communication to mislead the listener. At the very least, it might be pretentious nonsense. Don't fall for it.

Let's take a closer look.

Think of someone you consider an expert. Try to score them using this scale. A zero means you know zilch about this expert, making it hard to judge whether they can be trusted.

A score of +1 means you know a little about the expert, enough to lean toward trusting them.

A score of +5 means you know enough about the expert to fully trust them.

A score of −1 means that what little you know about the expert causes you to raise an eyebrow.

A score of −5 means you know enough about the expert to know they're not trustworthy at all.

Basically, the higher the score, the more you know about the expert. And the sign corresponds to whether this knowledge helps the expert's cause (+) or reveals them to be no expert at all (−).

Know and DIStrust   **Know and trust**

The head

−5   −4   −3   −2   −1   0   +1   +2   +3   +4   +5

The hands

−5   −4   −3   −2   −1   0   +1   +2   +3   +4   +5

The legs

−5   −4   −3   −2   −1   0   +1   +2   +3   +4   +5

The suit

−5   −4   −3   −2   −1   0   +1   +2   +3   +4   +5

From these ratings, you get a **profile of the expert**. It shows what info you're missing, what you have enough of, and lets you say with some confidence whether the expert's word is really worth anything.

The key word is "some." This method won't give you a definitive answer on whether to trust a specific expert, but it's sure to kickstart your critical thinking. It reduces your chances of being swayed by an incompetent expert or imposter.

Also, remember that your opinion about an expert should be based on facts and reasoning. The argument "I just don't like this expert, so I don't trust them" simply won't hold up.

They're the Boss! But Are They an Expert?

Imagine a school principal suddenly decides to change the school meal schedule and menu. They don't have a deep understanding of proper nutrition or how it affects children and teenagers. What they have instead is authority and the ability to issue orders. Can they be considered an expert?

○ Of course, since they're in charge.
○ I need more time to think about it.
○ I don't think so.

People might confuse influence with expertise. It often seems that someone who is in a higher position of power or has more authority must also know best. But is that always the case?

At school, students from different classes decided to form a soccer team. Since they didn't have a coach, the father of one of the boys stepped in to train them. He was a soccer fan, got along well with the teenagers, and became a real authority figure for them. They had to follow his orders and instructions. But they lost their first match... and then the next... and the next. After the fourth loss, the students began to question whether their coach actually knew how to train soccer players.

What if the principal ordered the school to exclusively serve burgers and energy drinks? Would you consider them an authority on the matter, even if their decision contradicts common sense and scientific principles of nutrition?

How to Survive a Zombie Apocalypse

Your city has been hit by a zombie apocalypse, and survivors have gathered in a shopping mall to figure out their next move. Among them are the mayor—a popular and respected figure—and a humble biology teacher from the local school.

The mayor, with all his authority and connections, proposes you stay put in the mall, fortify it, and wait for help to arrive. He confidently asserts that his leadership and management skills will save everyone, even though he knows next to nothing about zombies or viruses. His plan seems straightforward—stay in a safe place. He backs up his suggestion with a lot of loud enthusiasm and a lot of pressure.

The teacher is the complete opposite. She offers that you head to the nearest research center with a biology lab. She's got a background in virus research, knows the ins and outs of how viruses spread and how to fight them, and thinks she might be able to concoct an antidote. She's not making any promises, though, and has none of the mayor's flair for confidence.

The vote is down to you. What will you choose?

◯ Trust the authoritative and charismatic mayor, and stay with him in the shopping mall.

◯ Trust the timid teacher, who understands the problem despite lacking authority, and head with her to the lab.

This kind of thing is called a thought experiment. Discuss the situation with friends and family. Share your own opinion and listen to theirs. Talk about when it makes sense to follow someone who is in a higher position of authority and when it's better to follow someone who is more experienced and knowledgeable.

To Sum It Up, an Expert Is

Someone who:

- [ ] supports their opinion with facts and well-reasoned conclusions;
- [ ] can explain complex things in simple terms;
- [ ] admits their mistakes and inaccuracies;
- [ ] clearly understands what they are knowledgeable about and what they are not;
- [ ] doesn't necessarily appear confident;
- [ ] may not fit the typical image of a professional;
- [ ] isn't always in a position of power.

Or someone who:

- [ ] supports their opinion only with emotions and personal impressions;
- [ ] expresses themselves in convoluted ways;
- [ ] believes they never make mistakes in their conclusions;
- [ ] thinks their knowledge is exhaustive and final;
- [ ] always acts with self-assurance and unwavering confidence;
- [ ] strictly conforms to the typical image of a professional;
- [ ] possesses power and authority.

I AM AN EXPERT!
How to Find Arguments and Prove Your Point of View

We don't just consume information; we create it and share it with others. Critical thinking is just as valuable in this process, especially if you want to be a persuasive and responsible conversationalist, influencer, or someone's mentor—in other words, an **expert**. Think you can't do it? You definitely can! But first, take a moment to consider:

When can you show off your expertise?

When I...

- ☐ Present or give reports during school.
- ☐ Participate in community activities.
- ☐ Post and comment on social media.
- ☐ Get interviewed for a job.
- ☐ Help my younger sibling with their homework.
- ☐ Teach my parents about teen slang.
- ☐ _____
- ☐ _____
- ☐ _____
- ☐ _____

In life, there are many situations where taking on the role of an expert doesn't just give you an ego boost, but also matters to yourself and others.

How to Write a Helpful Review

Let's remind ourselves again how an expert opinion differs from run-of-the mill, everymen's opinions:

	Expert	~~Expert~~
Speaks more about their emotions and impressions than about facts.	☐	☐
Focuses more on facts than on their feelings.	☐	☐
Gives advice without any justification.	☐	☐
Supports their conclusions and advice with arguments.	☐	☐

A real expert always feels a sense of **responsibility** for what they write or say. They strive to understand in advance how their opinion might impact others.

Try writing a review of a movie, series, book, or game as an expert. Or maybe you just came back from a trip? Then try writing a review of your hotel or an attraction you visited. It doesn't matter if the review is positive or negative. Remember to write your review in a way that doesn't leave the reader wondering, "But why does the author think this?"

My review of _____

_____

_____

_____

_____

_____

_____

_____

_____

My rating: ☆☆☆☆☆

Share your review with a friend, acquaintance, or post it online. Look out for any questions from readers and if they think your opinion has a basis or not.

What Is an Argument?

How well-supported was your review? Whether we are convincing depends on our ability to choose strong arguments. **An argument** is an explanation that helps prove your point of view. Strong arguments are hard to undermine.

For example, say you and your friends are discussing how to spend time after school: shoot some hoops outside or game at home. You say, "Playing basketball is better because exercise and fresh air are good for your health." Everything that follows the word "because" makes up your argument. It's hard to challenge the statement that exercise is good for your health (unless you're a hard-core skeptic!).

> **Are arguments the same thing as facts?**
>
> Not necessarily. A fact can become an argument, but not all arguments need to be facts. Your arguments might include examples, well-known quotes, or references to personal experience.

There are people who get a kick out of questioning even the most rock-solid arguments. This is **radical skepticism** and has nothing to do with critical thinking.

Want a Dog? Convince Me!

Mary (14 years old) *really wanted to adopt a dog from the shelter, but her parents wouldn't let her. So Mary made a list of arguments to persuade her mom and dad. Which of these arguments would convince you if you were one of Mary's parents? And maybe this will motivate you to suggest bringing a pet home to your own family!*

- **Facts:** the expert's favorite tools.

    "Clive Wynn, a researcher at the University of Arizona, explains in his book Dog Is Love that dogs have a unique ability to form bonds across species, making them exceptionally loyal companions."

- **Real-Life examples:** memorable anecdotes that support your opinion, assessment, request, or recommendation.

    "My friend's parents let him get a dog, and now he spends all his time playing with it outside instead of in front of the computer."

- **Personal experience:** something from your own life that can add extra weight to your opinion.

    "When I visited the dog shelter, I could feel how sad and lonely the dogs were. It made me feel sad too, knowing I couldn't give them a home."

- **The opinion of another expert or well-known figure,** preferably someone who is authoritative in the eyes of your audience.

    "As Napoleon Bonaparte once said, 'If you do not like dogs, you do not like fidelity.'"

- **A reliable source of information** can also be a strong argument.

    "On the British Journal of Health Psychology website, there is an article listing the benefits of dogs for human health, both mental and physical."

- **A logical argument** is a conclusion based on the principles of logic.

    "*All parents care about their children's well-being. You are my parents. Therefore, you also care about my well-being. Getting a dog will make me happier."*

- **An ethical argument** is based on ethical rules, moral principles, or universal human values.

    "Adopting a dog from the shelter will make the world a better place. We have a duty to care for other living beings."

Are there any arguments among these that you disagree with?

An argument that supports the opposite of what someone is trying to prove is called a **counter-argument.**

An expert not only knows how to express an opinion but also how to **debate persuasively**—as long as they are a skilled speaker.

You don't always need to present a long list of arguments—quality over quantity. And how well your arguments are organized matters too.

The Architecture of Proof

An opinion that, instead of keeping it to yourself, you express publicly and argue—even in a small group—becomes a thesis. A published movie review is a **thesis**.

Explaining to your parents why you can't live without a dog is a thesis. When you tell your friends, "This teacher doesn't like us, but that one does," that's also a thesis, which should be backed up with evidence to avoid it being just an opinion.

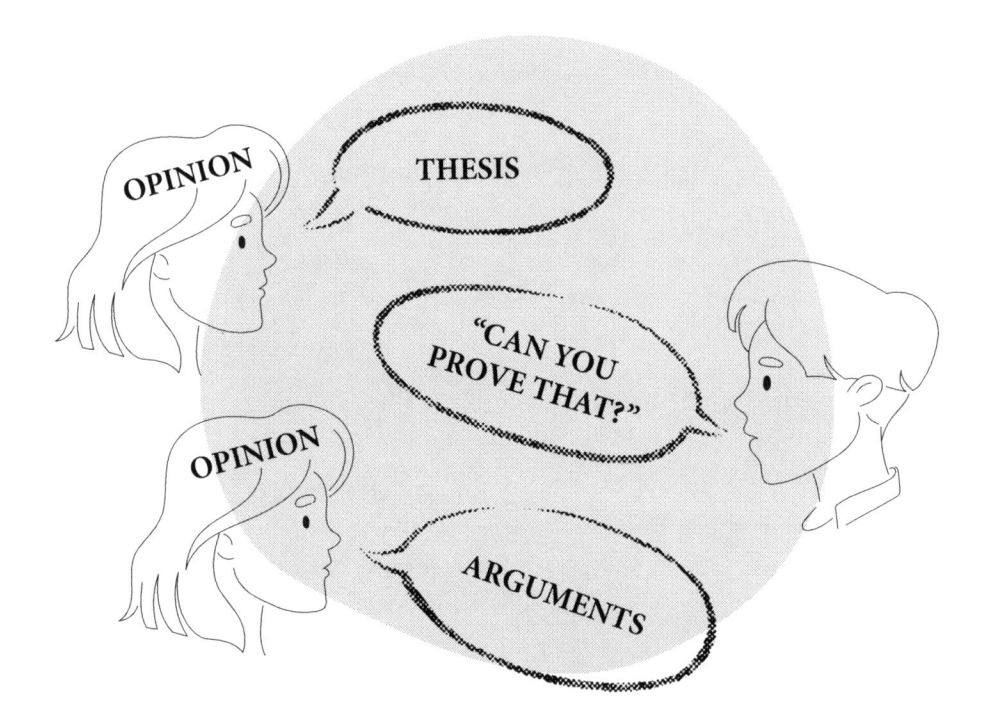

You already know that a thesis is supported by arguments. These arguments, like bricks, build the architecture of your proof. This structure can resemble a house, a tower, or a hut.

A—Argument
T—Thesis

It's important to not only know how to build the architecture of proof but also to recognize it around you—in books, articles, comments, and lectures.

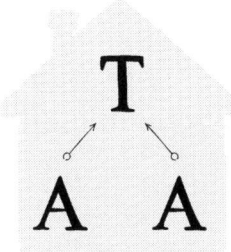

In this structure, each argument can be likened to a solid wall supporting your thesis. Even if one argument turns out to be weak or flawed, the others will continue to bolster your point. You might need two to five of these arguments.

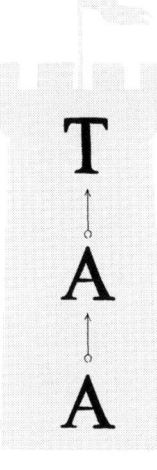

In the tower's case, arguments, like floors, follow a strict order and rely on each other. If one argument is weakened or flawed, all of the following arguments might topple over too.

As for the hut, it's a collection of branches and twigs—arguments that don't necessarily have an order, which would be weak on their own. However, piled together, they might just hold up... at least until a fierce wind starts to blow.

"Studies show that dogs are the most loyal animals. It's also proven that they have a positive impact on a person's emotional well-being. Finally, adopting a dog from a shelter will make the world a better place."

"It's proven that dogs positively impact emotional well-being. Therefore, if I had a dog, I would feel better overall. So, by getting me a dog, you guys would make me happier."

"My friend spent less time online after getting a dog. Visiting the shelter made me feel bad for all the animals. A dog could make me happier and guard the house."

What do you think is the most reliable method of argumentation, and which one is the weakest and most vulnerable?

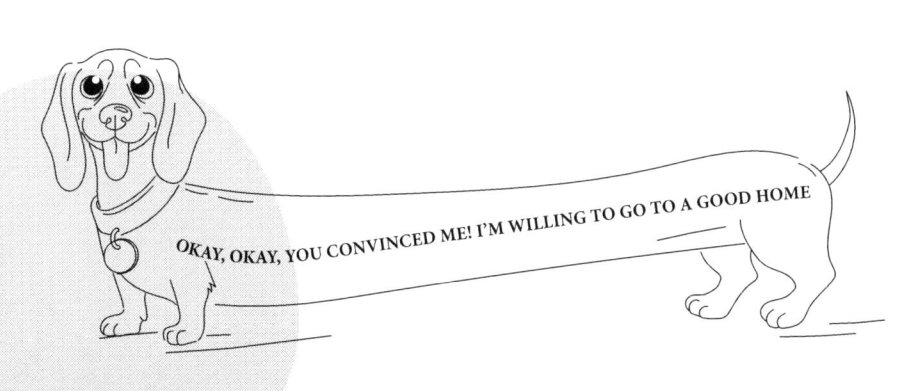

OKAY, OKAY, YOU CONVINCED ME! I'M WILLING TO GO TO A GOOD HOME

When might the ability to select and structure arguments come in handy?

When I...

☐ Participate in debates or discussions.
☐ Speak in public and present my ideas.
☐ Talk about my achievements during a job interview.
☐ Respond to comments on social media.
☐ --
☐ --
☐ --

A strong argument is like a ball you send flying straight into your opponent's goal. If you carefully plan a series of shots, there's a good chance at least one of them will score.

House, Tower, or Hut

Imagine you're at a youth science conference. Try to identify the structure of each presentation and decide on how well-argued it is.

Marina (14 years old):

"The climate is changing—global warming is really happening. Here's how I know that's true. The average air temperature has risen by 0.89°C over the last 100 years. The sea level is rising, deserts are expanding, and massive wildfires are occurring due to droughts. These changes intensified with the onset of the Industrial Revolution and accelerated significantly in the second half of the last century. The 20th century recorded the highest temperatures in the last 1,300 years. Therefore, global warming is not a myth, but a real threat to the planet."

○ House.   ○ Tower.   ○ Hut.

How well-argued do you think Marina's opinion (thesis) is?

○ There are enough arguments.   ○ There aren't enough arguments.

> Each of Marina's arguments is self-sufficient and bears weight, like a solid wall. Highlight each argument and count how many there are.

82

Peter (15 years old):

"I want to talk about why it's important to drink plenty of water. Doctors say that our health depends on the balance between salt and water in our body: if it's disrupted, our health worsens. Therefore, it's very important to maintain this balance at an optimal level. To do this, a person should drink an average of half an ounce to an ounce of water per pound of body weight per day. I recommend always carrying a bottle of water with you!"

◯ House. ◯ Tower. ◯ Hut.

How well-argued do you think Peter's opinion (thesis) is?

◯ There are enough arguments. ◯ There aren't enough arguments.

Do you feel the urge to contradict any of these arguments? Or maybe you'd like to see for yourself if the presenters' opinions are accurate?

> Peter's arguments are structured like floors—each one depends on the one before it. Highlight each argument and count how many there are.

How to Prepare Your Argumentation

Now it's your turn!

What viewpoint about an issue would you like to share with others—your followers, friends, teachers, or parents?

> Strong arguments don't always come to mind immediately. Sometimes you need to prepare by searching for them. This is especially significant if you're giving an important speech or want to write a very convincing post.

Formulate a thesis (statement) and follow these four simple steps:

1. **Find some strong arguments and write them down on a separate piece of paper.** For instance, you might include verified facts and persuasive examples. Remember or refer back to the different types of arguments you can use.

2. **Review your arguments to ensure they can be constructed, like bricks, into a house or tower.** If the arguments are too different or don't quite fit together—no problem. Let it be a hut, but in that case, make sure you have a hefty pile of sticks! There's nothing stopping you from mixing and matching different argumentation styles!

3. **Check whether you were able to structure your arguments logically and persuasively.** Put yourself in the shoes of your audience and try to spot any inconsistencies or weak points in your evidence. Assess how convincing it is from another person's perspective.

4 **Write your speech, message, post, or request.** First, state your opinion (thesis). Then, present the arguments in the necessary order and draw a conclusion in favor of this opinion. If you need a reference, see how Marina and Peter did it.

Yay! Now you'll at least speak convincingly. But prepare yourself ahead of time for when you'll have to… admit that you're wrong.

Admit That I'm Wrong!?

When your conversation partner is another expert with a different viewpoint, you have to be ready for a real battle of wits and challenging discussion. Just make sure it's a civilized conversation, not a fight.

Preparing to admit you're wrong in advance doesn't mean throwing your opinion to the wind. It means telling yourself: "My opinion is important to me. I have arguments in its favor. But what if I'm mistaken?"

	Discussion	Fight
Each person wants to be understood but doesn't really care about understanding the other.	☐	☐
Each person wants not only to be understood but also to understand the other as well as possible.	☐	☐
Each person tries to influence the other through emotions, mutual accusations, and pressing on each other's pain points.	☐	☐
Each person tries to argue their opinion and consider the other's words with a clear mind.	☐	☐
The people involved are usually not willing to change their opinion or admit their mistakes.	☐	☐
The people involved can change their opinion and admit mistakes if the other person's arguments are stronger and more convincing.	☐	☐

The last point is especially important (remember Socrates!). An honest expert won't heatedly defend their opinion if they realize their arguments are lacking or if they internally agree with their opponent.

If you find yourself in that situation, you can say, "You have some great arguments! It's hard to disagree with them," or "Your evidence is quite convincing, I'm going to take your opinion into consideration." This will allow you to maintain your integrity by acknowledging the validity of the other person's points and also demonstrate intellectual flexibility.

I Am an Expert Because...

It's time to test your knowledge.

Mark which of these are traits of an expert.

- [ ] I am knowledgeable about certain topics.
- [ ] I can share my knowledge with others.
- [ ] I know how to explain and argue my opinions.
- [ ] I take responsibility for persuading others.
- [ ] I can turn a fight into a reasoned discussion.
- [ ] I understand that I can be wrong even in my own field.
- [ ] I can change my opinion if a better argument is presented.

There's no quick and easy way to become a true expert. It takes gathering knowledge, gaining experience, and practicing argumentation.

So, if you left some of the points above unmarked, that's alright. Even just by looking at them, you're identifying the areas you can grow in.

If you can't convince someone even with thorough argumentation, don't blame yourself. Some people are stubbornly unwilling to change their mind, even when contrary evidence is staring them right in the face.

HOW CRITICAL THINKING HELPS YOU LEARN AND GROW

When you're learning, new information transforms into knowledge, beliefs, views, and skills. The quality of this information determines what you will know and be able to do. Critical thinking acts as a filter that helps you sift out useless or harmful nonsense from information that is valuable for your development.

What to Learn About

People have accumulated an incredible amount of knowledge about the world. And we're only continuing to discover and create more at an ever-growing rate. Some things you already know, while others you may want to learn. To understand what to spend time learning about, you can map out your **circles of knowledge**.

→ **EVERYTHING THAT CAN BE KNOWN**

→ **EVERYTHING I WANT TO KNOW**

→ **EVERYTHING I ALREADY KNOW**

What do you think lies beyond the circle of "everything that can be known"?

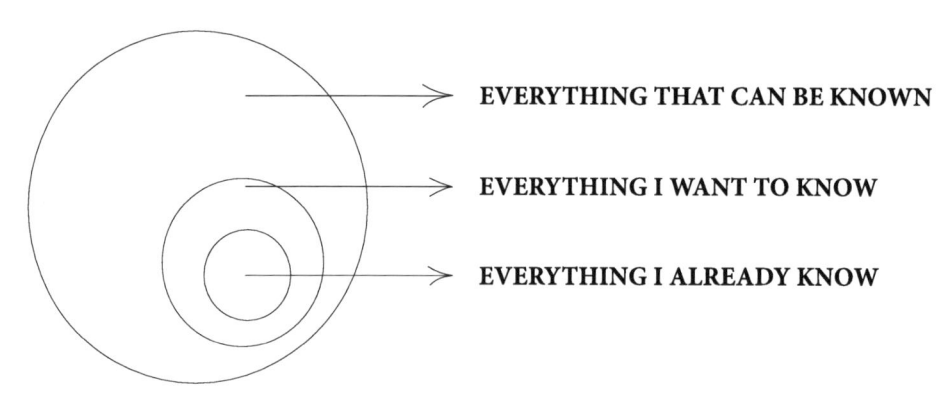

The first circle—everything you already know and can do. This is your starting point for determining what to pursue next. Choose a topic or profession and briefly list what you already know and can do in that area.

- -

- -

- -

- -

It's important to accurately define the scope of your knowledge and skills.

You can do this in several ways:

- **Take a look at your achievements and awards.** Don't worry, if you've never won a medal or earned a title, that doesn't mean you have no knowledge or skills. It might just be that you haven't had the chance to test them in a contest or competition.

- **Tackle additional trials and tests.** However, not all knowledge can be assessed using tests, and most skills can't be measured this way at all. In these cases, you can come up with a challenge!

- **Ask for the opinion of someone who can evaluate you objectively.** This could be a teacher, coach, more experienced peer, or adult. Ideally, this person is—you guessed it—an expert themselves.

- **Compare your knowledge and skills with those of an expert.** Just don't go overboard with this, so you don't get discouraged. Anyone who knows and can do more than you is a great example and motivation to keep striving, not a reason to throw in the towel. That's why it's best to only make comparisons along the lines of "I can do this—they can do this" and "I know this—they know this."

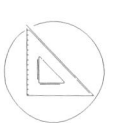

The second circle—everything you want to know and be able to do.
Once you've identified what you already know and can do, it's easier to understand what you're missing. Try to write down what else you want to know and be able to do in your chosen topic or area.

As you learn and grow, the second circle turns into the first—everything you wanted to know and be able to do, you begin to know and be able to do. You will read about how to plan your learning and development in the chapters on systematic and strategic thinking.

When a person underestimates their own knowledge and abilities, it gives way to **imposter syndrome**. Being praised for their expertise and skills makes them feel insecure and ashamed—they believe they don't deserve the recognition and are taking the place of someone more qualified.

That begs the question: What happens to someone who thinks they're better than they actually are?

Even if you want to start a topic from scratch, you can still try to identify your launch point—anything that you already know, however little.

The third circle—everything that can possibly be known and mastered in a particular topic or field of knowledge. For example, in programming, design, mathematics, or photography.

Knowledge gathers and expands at a rate that's nearly impossible to keep up with, so knowing everything is probably an unworthy goal. However, it's valuable to periodically peer into this circle to understand what else is out there to learn.

Where to Learn

When you're choosing courses or selecting a school, you won't get far—or where you want to go—without critical thinking.

Which of these students applied critical thinking to their online course selection?

Mark (15 years old) decided to learn programming. After all, that's the most promising and high-paying profession (according to his friend)!

He happened upon an ad for a programming school for teens while scrolling through social media. Without thinking about it too much, he signed up and asked his parents to pay for the first lessons.

At first, Mark was full of enthusiasm. But after a few classes, he realized that the course was designed for those who already had some knowledge of the subject, unlike Mark, who didn't know the first thing about programming.

Mark ended up dropping the course. It only took a few weeks of wasted time and a hefty bill to realize it wasn't for him.

Several teachers suggested that creative Elena (15 years old) take an interior design course because it was a lucrative skill.

Elena decided to check for herself if that was true. Turns out, her teachers' perspective on this topic—like many others—was slightly outdated; Elena found research papers and articles that suggested interior designers might soon be replaced by AI.

After thinking it over, Elena decided that she still wanted to take design courses—not to make money, but explore a potential passion.

She made a list of 10 online schools, carefully studied the programs of each, read student reviews, and chose a course at a school that she believed offered the most reliable and high-quality education.

Critical thinking ◯ On ◯ Off

Critical thinking ◯ On ◯ Off

What mistakes do you think Mark made, unlike Elena?

Write those mistakes down so you can avoid them when choosing a source for your own learning. Don't be like Mark.

- -

- -

- -

- -

> When reading reviews about courses, online schools, or universities, remember to pay attention to facts and arguments.

And what information would you or do you typically look for when choosing where to study?

- [ ] How the curriculum is structured.
- [ ] Who the instructors are.
- [ ] What the reviews of the course say.
- [ ] What publications exist about the organization offering the course.
- [ ] How the organization is ranked among other offline or online schools.
- [ ] _____
- [ ] _____
- [ ] _____
- [ ] _____

Struggling to evaluate the course? If possible, show it to an expert you know in the field you're interested in (this could be one of your teachers) and ask what they think about the program and whether it fits your goals.

> You will read about how to set learning goals in the chapters on systematic and strategic thinking.

Who to Learn From

From an expert, duh! I think you didn't need me to tell you that. In one of the previous sections, you saw a detailed guide on how to evaluate an expert "from head to toe" and tell the real deal apart from a con man.

> **If an expert messes up, should you stop trusting them?**
>
> Every expert has their own areas of knowledge. The first circle, "Everything I already know," is broader for an expert in a particular area than for most people. However, even they have gaps—things they don't know or can't do yet. So, yes, experts make mistakes too. If an expert **acknowledges their mistake**, they are open to new knowledge and won't intentionally mislead you. However, if they refuse to admit obvious mistakes and inaccuracies, you should probably take their word with a grain of salt... or even several grains.

How to Learn

Learning while using critical thinking and information means:

- 1. Understanding what information you need.
- 2. Searching for and finding that information.
- 3. Analyzing and verifying the information.
- 4. Memorizing the information.
- 5. Applying the information to your life.

All these items are stages in the process of learning any knowledge or skill.

If you're traveling somewhere and decide to skip a turn here and a step there, you won't get to your destination. Learning is no different.

For example, what would happen if you started with the second stage?

And what about if you skipped the third stage?

Learning is a step-by-step process. If you decide to freestyle it, it can really hurt your results.

To understand what information you need, refer back to the circle of "Everything I want to know and be able to do."

*You can read about **strategies for finding information** on page 13.*

*Instructions on how to **analyze and verify information** are on page 50.*

How to Dodge Thinking Traps

There are several thinking traps that can mess with your ability to find and understand information, learn new knowledge, and develop skills. You might not even know when you fall into one.

Draw a checkmark if you've ever stepped in similar traps.

○ **Just one click away!**

When Anya searches for study materials online, she only opens the first link that appears in the search results. That one's the top result, so reading anything else is unnecessary, right?

○ **Too long, didn't read.**

Moisha has no problem scanning Instagram captions and news headlines. However, reading the entire article is... a whole different matter. Don't even ask about textbooks—he thinks they're too long and dense, so doesn't even bother trying.

○ **Follow the crowd!**

Zuri and Kyle only watch the shows their friends are watching, read books that are popular on TikTok, follow health regimens recommended by the biggest online gurus, and trust experts everyone always references... Sensing a pattern here?

○ **If I disagree, it must be wrong!**

Eileen reads an article claiming that pineapple belongs on pizza, but since she firmly believes it's an abomination, she immediately dismisses it as fake news. Later, she stumbles upon a study "proving" that coffee drinkers are smarter, and she eagerly shares it with everyone, feeling validated as she sips her third cup of the day.

○ **Authorities are always right!**

Sonia believes that if a well-known and authoritative person says or writes something, it can't possibly be wrong or misleading. This even extends to actors wearing white coats in cosmetics ads.

○ **If I fail, it's the end of the world!**

Damien's stomach feels like it's going to flip inside out, just like it always does before an exam. He thinks that if he doesn't pass, his life will fall apart. He'll flunk out of school, never get a real job, and his parents will probably disown him!

The fancy name for thinking traps is "**cognitive biases**."

Many of them are a result of **intellectual laziness**, which, if you remember, is when you don't want to put in the mental effort to think critically.

○ **Going down with the ship.**

Ollie joined a gymnastics team. Six months of painfully aching muscles and leotard shame went by before they decided it wasn't for them. But what about the evenings they spent learning how to somersault that they can't get back? And the money their parents paid for classes? They can't quit now...

This applies to everyone!

○ Rakesh shocked his parents by announcing he wasn't planning on going to college at all. Don't worry, mom and dad, your son read online that some of the richest people on the planet dropped out! He, too, is going to be a world-famous billionaire without higher education!

I made a mistake so I am a mistake.

○ Antoine's face falls as he reads the email saying he didn't get the lifeguarding job he applied for. "I'm horrible at interviewing," he sighs. "I'm totally incompetent." Last week he lost his keys and has been beating himself up for how forgetful he is. Two weeks ago he and his girlfriend got into a fight, and he decided he must be unlovable. Poor Antoine. He really needs a hug.

Think about what advice you could give each of these people to help free them from these traps. We'll limit ourselves to one piece of advice: Always look out for these thinking traps as you walk through life so you don't happen to fall in.

It's easier to avoid traps and correct cognitive errors when you know what they might be and how they can hinder your learning.

Your Personal Knowledge Inventory

Keep your critical thinking sharp during your studies with a journal. Consider starting one either in a physical notebook or a note-taking app.

When you learn something new, crack it open and jot down brief answers to the following questions:

What did you learn?
Write one or two sentences about what you were able to learn or discover. This could be a new fact, term, method, technique, theory, or concept.

From where?
Specify the exact source of the information. This is important so you can find it again if needed or reference it in discussion for increased credibility.

How reliable is this source or expert?
Score the reliability of the information source or briefly characterize the expert.

Where will this be useful?
For example, in your work or hobbies. Or maybe your relationships and studies. Understanding the value of new knowledge and achievements can motivate you to keep learning.

Do I want to learn more about this?
If yes, what specifically? This will help you fill up the second circle of your knowledge, "Everything I want to know and be able to do."

Have I fallen into a thinking trap?
Thinking traps can affect the conclusions you draw from new knowledge, and your assessment of its accuracy, usefulness, and applicability. Also, falling into a thinking trap might lead you to misjudge your abilities and stop wanting to learn.

It's helpful to answer these questions every time you learn something new. After all, a good question is the sharpest lens for critical thinking! Plus, this practice will help you remember and recall the most important things you've learned with more ease.

You might be thinking we forgot something. There is one more crucial question: Why learn in the first place? We'll explore the answer to this in the chapter on strategic thinking.

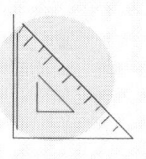

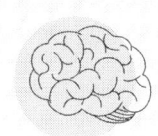

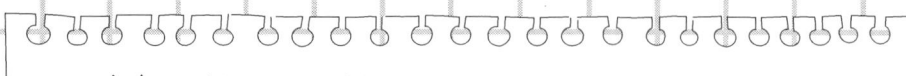

Victor, 16 years old

Learned how to take cool backlit portraits on the phone.

Watched a YouTube video from a photography channel.

The expert seems okay—a professional photographer who teaches at a photography school. He has a great portfolio and good reviews.

Now I can take awesome photos for my social media, maybe even earn money by taking portraits.

I want to learn more about how to use different phone camera modes for creative shooting.

Orla, 15 years old

Just learned about this football tactic called the "false nine." It's when the striker drops back, creating space and confusing the other team's defense.

Read about it on a sports site, then we talked about it at practice.

The site's all about football, with interviews from pros, so I trust it.

Gonna try it out in our next school games with the girls' team. It might really step up our game. Now I'm curious about other tactics and how to use them better in matches. I want to learn more about this stuff.

Pilar, 15 years old

Heard that if you eat just fruit for five days straight, you can lose weight fast without hurting your health, then start building muscle.

Saw it in a video from this popular influencer. But, even though he's got a lot of followers, he's not a doctor or an actual trainer. He didn't share any research or expert opinions to back up what he was saying.

I'm thinking this advice isn't really useful for me. Not sure a diet like that would be good. Definitely need to double-check this.

Now I want to learn more about balanced diets and ones that are actually safe and effective if you're getting into sports.

I just realized that I almost fell into the trap of thinking a popular blogger is an expert!

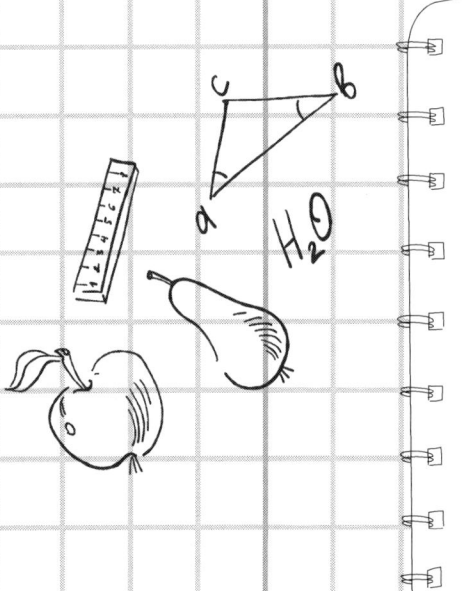

What's holding me back from reaching my goals and getting results?

What do I want to pursue in the future?

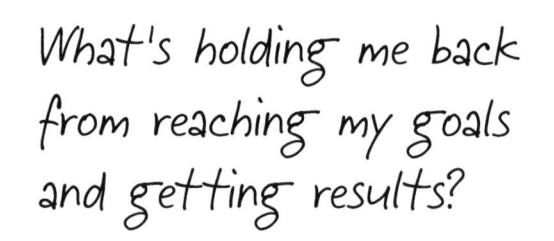

What do I lose by working toward my goals?

I THINK LIKE A STRATEGIST
I learn, grow, and choose my career using strategic thinking

How do I figure out what I'm passionate about?

What should I direct my resources towards?

Do I even have goals? If so, what are they?

Can I change my interests at any point?

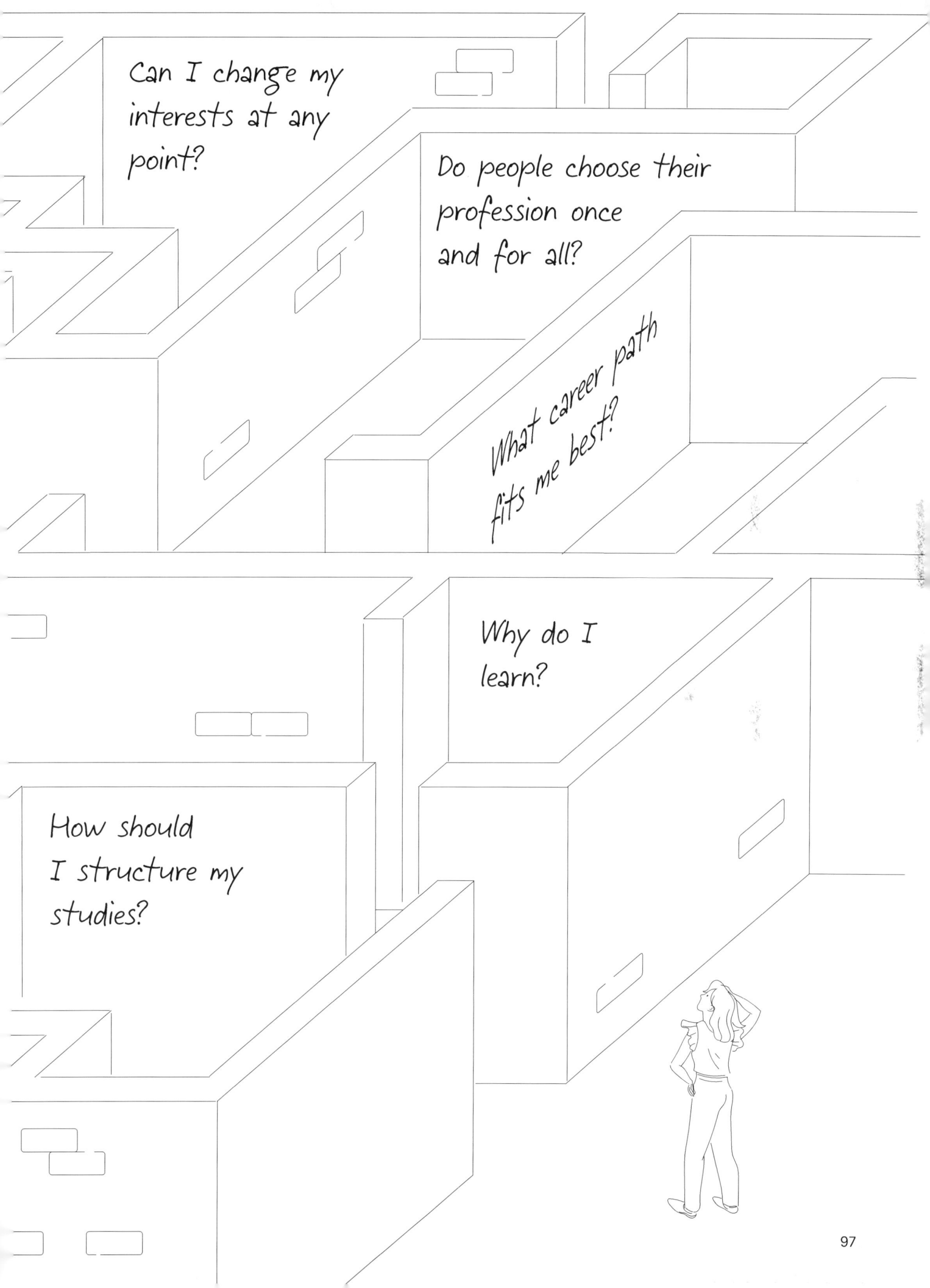

Do people choose their profession once and for all?

What career path fits me best?

Why do I learn?

How should I structure my studies?

WHAT IS STRATEGIC THINKING AND WHY DO YOU NEED IT?

Strategic thinking helps you move forward, make changes in yourself, and influence the world around you. Whether you want to become a successful entrepreneur, win a cooking competition, or build a romantic relationship with someone, having a good strategy is essential.

Strategy—Your Way to Reach the Future You Want

It's like seeing yourself and your life from a future perspective. Strategy helps you overcome challenges and not get stuck in the daily grind. It shows not only what you want to achieve but also how you're going to get there.

Let's say you dream of saving the planet from pollution. A clean and livable Earth is your dream future. But how will you move toward it? At the very least, you can start by cutting out single-use plastic packaging today. If you're thinking bigger, you could dive into chemistry, make it your career, and invent a method to break down plastic. Or maybe you'll become a biologist and grow bacteria that eat different types of waste. And there are countless other ways you can contribute to achieving that future.

The vision of the future you want for yourself, others, or the planet, and your path to get there—that's what strategy is all about. That's why it's like a map.

> There are some goals that can only be achieved through teamwork. In those cases, strategy becomes what brings people together.

Let's Play?

Imagine you're going on a trip. Come up with names for the starting point A and the destination B—they can be any cities, countries, or even continents.

My starting point (A) _

My destination (B) _

If your destination isn't just down the street, you'll have a long journey with several stops along the way—these are marked by other points. Flip the page and try to map out your route—connect points A, B, and the intermediate stops with a line.

But there are a few catches:

1. There must be at least three intermediate stops.
2. Avoid stops at the symbol ☠.
3. Each stop at a symbol 🕒 will add an extra day to your journey.
4. You can't spend more than one extra day.
5. And you can't spend more than 100 🏛 on the trip.

And don't forget to turn on your hawk-like attention!

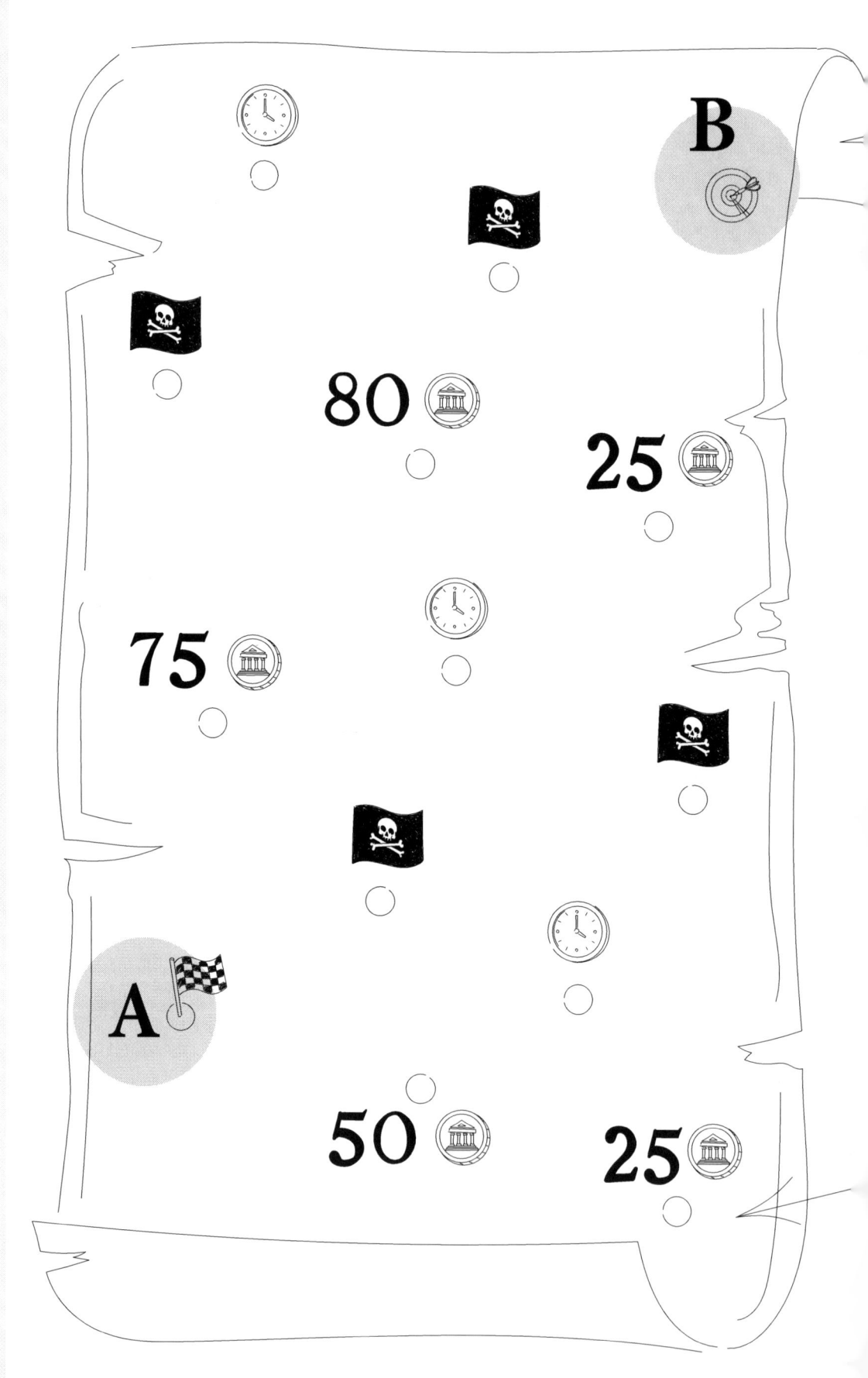

Copy this map and ask one of your friends or family members to chart their own path based on the given conditions. Then compare your routes to see if they match.

Feel free to come up with your own version of this game!

Were you able to complete the task? Way to go, I believed in you all along. Now, try to map out another possible route. Just remember the conditions of your journey!

The Elements of a Strategy

To craft a strategy, it's imperative to know what elements it consists of. Take another look at the drawing and try to figure out what's what in the strategy—what's the **goal**, what are the **threats**, what are the losses, and what are the **resources**?

🎯 is the goal.

🏴‍☠️ is _____

🕙 is _____

🏛 is _____

Also, when creating a strategy, you have to understand the conditions you'll be working under and where to start. Sometimes one circumstantial change is enough for the whole strategy to need reworking.

For example, try to map out a route that uses as few resources 🏛 as possible, makes at least three stops, and doesn't take more than one extra day.

Did it work? Here's a new challenge—you can pass through the spots marked 🏴‍☠️, but each stop there increases the risk of being robbed of 50 🏛. You still need to complete the route without spending more than 100 🏛. total. The other conditions stay the same. Find a new path!

And what if your starting point changes? Let's say your journey now begins in the bottom right corner. Will that affect your strategy?

The goal is what you're aiming to achieve.

Losses are what you might have to deliberately sacrifice along the way.

Threats are anything that could get in the way of reaching your goal—setbacks, difficulties, dangers, and risks.

Resources are what you need to achieve your goal.

The Map of My Life

We need strategies not just for games or saving the planet.

In everyday life, a good strategy helps us:

- [ ] Understand what we want from the future.
- [ ] Achieve our goals.
- [ ] Account for threats and inevitable losses.
- [ ] Use resources wisely.
- [ ] Plan specific steps.

And it doesn't matter whether you're planning a trip, looking for a side gig, or deciding which college to attend. As soon as you have a big goal in the future, you need a strategy to reach it.

> **Is strategy the same as a tactic?**
>
> No, but nice try. A **strategy** for achieving a major life goal is usually planned over years or even decades. For example, getting into your dream school, finding a job, or starting a romantic relationship.
> A **tactic**, on the other hand, is the specific steps you take on that lengthy journey to your goal. For instance, passing a chemistry exam is a tactic, while becoming a microbiologist is the strategy.

"I've set a goal to run six miles in six months. First, I'm going to assess my current fitness level. Then, I'll figure out a good diet and workout routine. I'll start by gradually increasing my distance and working on my stamina. There's a chance the weather might mess up my training, so I'll need a backup plan for indoor workouts. I'll have to give up some free time and skip the donuts. Also, I need to get some decent running shoes!"
(Felipe, 15 years old)

Different people may use different strategies to achieve similar goals. Each person has their own starting point, resources, potential losses, and threats. So, blindly copying other people's strategies typically isn't a good move.

What in Felipe's strategy qualifies as threats, losses, and resources?

And what goal are you working toward right now?

Write down a meaningful goal for yourself and outline a strategy for achieving it.

My goal is _____

First, I plan on _____
_____

Then, I will _____
_____
_____
_____

I will need _____
_____

I'll have to sacrifice _____
or say no to _____
_____

I might be hindered by _____
_____
_____

Resources aren't just money and objects. They can include knowledge, time, support from loved ones—anything that helps you get where you wanna go.

What's similar between this strategy and the map from the game above?

There can be several different paths to achieving a goal, remember?

SMART Goals

A goal is the endpoint you're trying to reach, where you achieve what you want. Defining this destination is where strategy begins.

The path to your goal can be either short and quick or long and winding.

103

Sometimes that depends on how well you define your goal.

SMART goals are:

SMART is an acronym, and the letters stand for:

S—specific.

M—measurable.

A—achievable.

R—relevant.

T—time-bound.

Setting goals in this way means they are well-thought-out and more likely to come to fruition, making them smart!

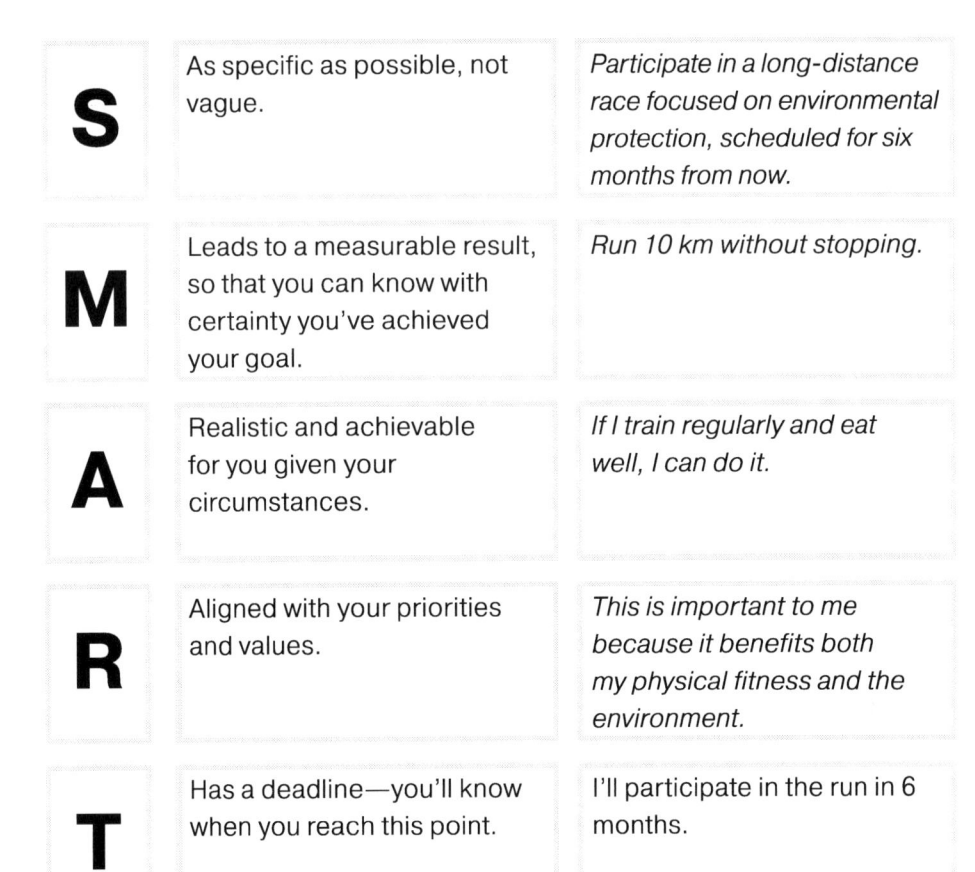

S	As specific as possible, not vague.	*Participate in a long-distance race focused on environmental protection, scheduled for six months from now.*
M	Leads to a measurable result, so that you can know with certainty you've achieved your goal.	*Run 10 km without stopping.*
A	Realistic and achievable for you given your circumstances.	*If I train regularly and eat well, I can do it.*
R	Aligned with your priorities and values.	*This is important to me because it benefits both my physical fitness and the environment.*
T	Has a deadline—you'll know when you reach this point.	*I'll participate in the run in 6 months.*

How can I tell if my goal is realistic and achievable?

A realistic goal is one that can be accomplished under ideal conditions. For example, getting into the best university in Tokyo. That's realistic, right? Yes, but everyone has different circumstances, resources, challenges, and sacrifices to make. These factors determine whether a goal is achievable within the timeframe you've set. Some people have been to Japan and are familiar with the language and culture. Some already live in Tokyo. For others, getting to Japan might be too expensive, so they'll need to save up for a ticket and housing first. So, while a goal might be realistic in general, it could be difficult for a specific person to achieve.

Check if the goal you wrote down on page 103 is SMART:

		Yes	No
S	Is it as specific as possible?	☐	☐
M	Does it have a measurable result?	☐	☐
A	Is it achievable for me specifically?	☐	☐
R	Is it important to me?	☐	☐
T	Does it have a deadline?	☐	☐

The more affirmative answers you have, the better your goal is formulated. If it's hard to say "yes" to some questions right now, it might be worth reconsidering your goal and making some adjustments.

Strategic Plan

A carefully constructed strategy becomes a strategic plan, meaning a plan that covers a significant period of time and outlines the steps to achieve your goal stage by stage.

Do you think Felipe's marathon training strategy already sounds like a concrete plan?

○ Yes, it sounds like a plan with deadlines.
○ It doesn't really seem like a plan yet.
○ I'm not sure.

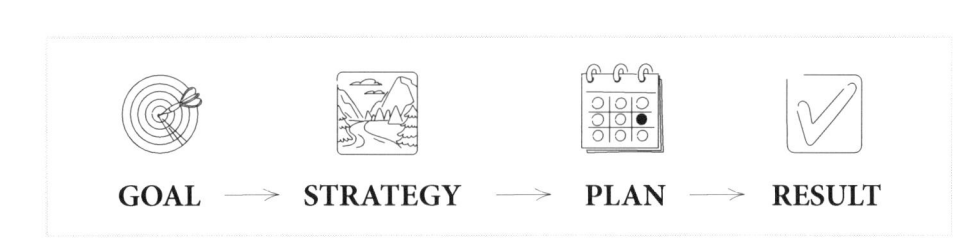

GOAL → STRATEGY → PLAN → RESULT

It's possible that Felipe's strategy is missing something that would make it into a plan.

A strategy starts looking like a plan when:

☐ All stages are described in the order they need to be completed.
☐ Each stage has a specific deadline.
☐ The deadlines for each stage are marked on a calendar.

People who think strategically usually don't stop at just one plan—they've got backups! You've got your main plan, but then there's a Plan B (and maybe even a Plan C) in case things go sideways—whether it's a change in conditions, unexpected hurdles, or resources running low. Or maybe Plan A is just asking for too much sacrifice. Better to be overprepared, right?

In your opinion, could a strategy really work and lead to your goal, if it's not transformed into a plan?

105

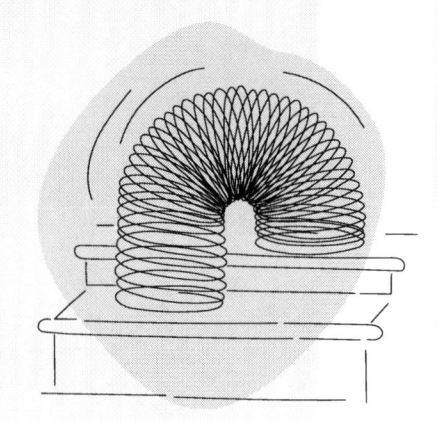

Can you change your strategy and plan?

Sometimes, it's absolutely necessary—when the conditions for reaching your goal change, new resources become available, or, on the contrary, if resources run out sooner than expected. There could also be unforeseen threats that were difficult to anticipate when the strategy and plan were created. Strategic thinking must also be flexible!

When to Strategize (and When to Wing It)

If we planned out every single step of our lives, it'd be a snoozefest. So, it's crucial to leave some room for spontaneity. Only you can decide when you need a strategy and when you can just go with the flow.

There are exceptions, of course. Some people devise detailed strategies for things like cleaning the house or grocery shopping. These mini-strategies can come in handy too.

I need a strategy when…

Studying for an exam.

I want to improve my health.

I don't need a strategy when…

Hanging out with my friends.

I want to make lunch.

There's no need to overcomplicate the everyday stuff. Save the strategic thinking for those completely novel, long-term goals where the road ahead is still uncharted.

Let's Wrap It Up, Shall We?

Strategic thinking is the ability to:

	X	V
Set goals and figure out the best ways to achieve them.	☐	☐
Consider the factors that affect reaching your goals.	☐	☐
Assess potential threats and sacrifices along the way.	☐	☐
Manage your resources wisely to meet your objectives.	☐	☐
Plan your actions ahead of time.	☐	☐
Set clear, long-term goals.	☐	☐
Be flexible with your plans and strategies.	☐	☐
Go with your gut without any goal or plan.	☐	☐
Take risks without thinking about the consequences.	☐	☐
Never alter your strategy.	☐	☐
Exactly replicate others' strategies and plans.	☐	☐
Stick rigidly to one plan and never adjust it.	☐	☐

HOW TO PICK A CAREER YOU'LL ACTUALLY LOVE

Strategic thinking helps you connect today to tomorrow—the starting pistol to the finish line. So, what kind of journey is choosing and pursuing a career like?

- [ ] Like a steady, straight climb up a mountain.
- [ ] Like a journey through the hills, with its peaks and valleys.
- [ ] Like wandering through a forest full of winding paths and forks.
- [ ] Like _____

This journey is different for everyone. Will it lead to the outcome you dream of? Will it get you where you want to go? That largely depends on the quality of your strategy!

To Choose or Not to Choose

Remember the game where you had to connect Point A to Point B (page 100)? When you're choosing a career, the starting point marks your initial opportunities. The ending point is your future profession. Or one of your professions.

Before charting the path from A to B, it's imperative to understand how compatible they are.

Would someone who practically melts and immediately burns under scorching sunlight (Point A) want to travel to the Sahara Desert (Point B)? Probably not. On the other hand, if basking in the sun is your thing, you might think twice before packing your warmest coat and moving to the Arctic.

Picking a profession is just the same—you're deciding what kind of lifestyle you want to lead.

Is it your life-long dream to study hard and secure a job you absolutely despise?

○ I wouldn't call it that, but I will if I have to...
○ No, I don't want that.
○ What? No! Never!

"Have"s and "should"s point to a lack of free will. And if there's no free will, there won't be any strategy, either. That's probably not a good mentality to approach building your future with, wouldn't you say?

> The strategy involved in choosing a career is way different from most everyday strategies in your life. It can impact your life on a much larger scale—think decades!

The Starting Line

Point A isn't just the starting point of your journey. It's also the moment when you decide where you want to go. To choose your direction wisely, look inside yourself and identify your interests, values, and desires. You are your own best compass!

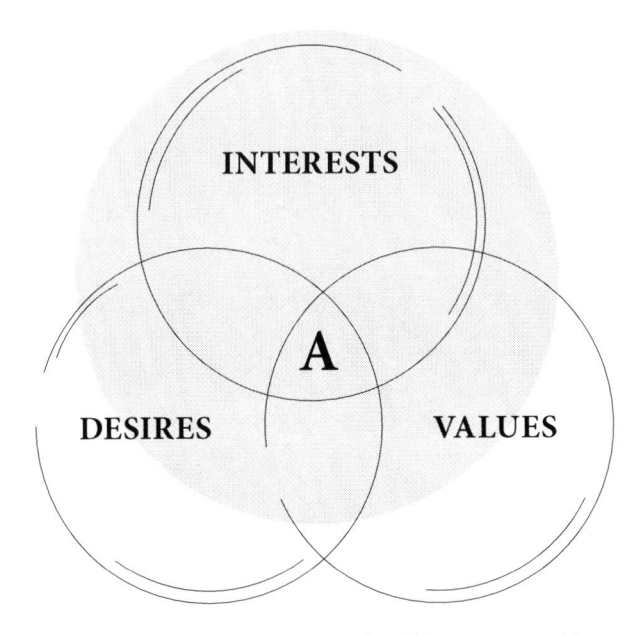

Interests are things you enjoy doing.

Desires are things you want to spend most of your time on.

Values are things you find most significant and live for.

Even if you're already breezing through your career journey like it's nothing, it can still be helpful to check in with your interests, desires, and values to make sure you don't want to change course.

INTERESTS / DESIRES / VALUES — A

Try to describe where you are in life currently:

Right now I'm most interested in _____

Right now I want to spend most of my time on _____

Right now it matters to me to _____

Now zoom out and look for connections between your interests, desires, and values. That combination might just become your push-off point.

You might end up with more than one match, so make sure to jot each one down:

I want to do _____,
because it interests me, and I think it's important.

I want to do _____,
because it interests me, and I think it's important.

I want to do _____,
because it interests me, and I think it's important.

Picture yourself in the future, knee-deep in what currently feels exciting, desirable, and important. Then ask yourself:

Do I still want to be doing this?
Am I still interested in it?
Do I still think it's important?

Contemplate these questions, looking through the rear view mirror of time.

> **Do your abilities matter when choosing a career path?**
>
> Your abilities are your internal resources. They can affect how quickly you reach your goals and what the results will be. People approach this in varying ways. Some choose a profession based on their current abilities. Others, on the contrary, develop abilities to fit their desired profession. There's also another method—choosing a career that aligns with the abilities you want to develop in the future. Many skills can be developed and refined throughout your life.

If what you want to spend time on genuinely interests you and feels important, it's worth considering whether it could become your profession.

Over time, your interests, desires, and values may change. A good career choice strategy should account for this possibility.

Knowing your abilities can help you guess which activities might come more naturally to you. However, this doesn't mean you have to turn them into your profession.

111

B, C, or D...

After determining your starting point and visualizing your future, mentally draw a line from point A to point B—connect your interests, desires, and values to a potential profession.

But there might be several professions that seem like a great fit for you. So, rather than just heading to one destination, you'll have a whole itinerary on your hands.

Write down and add on as many options as you consider necessary.

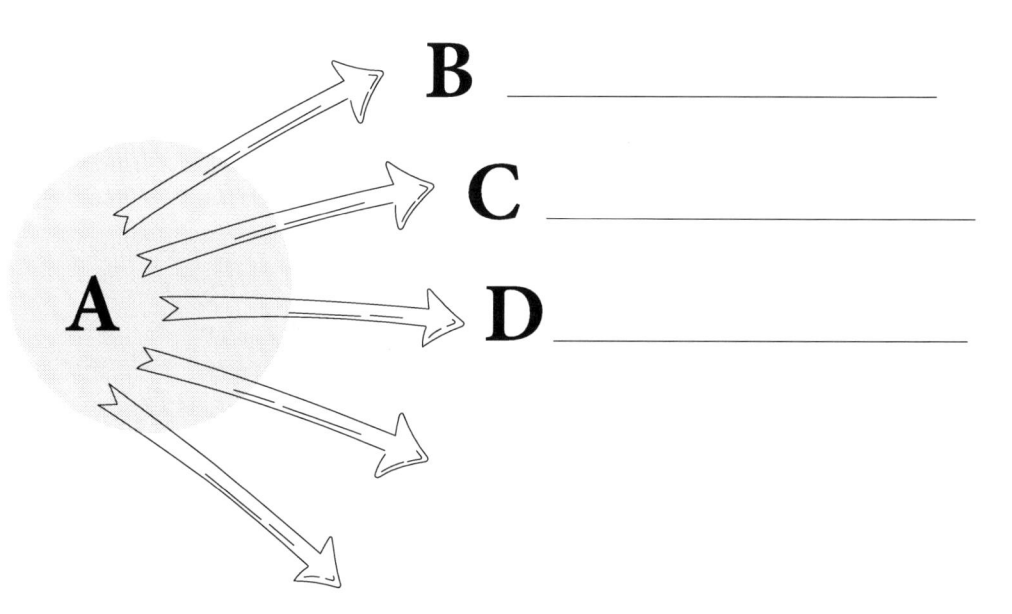

B _____

C _____

D _____

A

> Life is not a game where the winning options are predetermined. You can't be certain your choice is the correct one, or if the move you're about to make will cost you your victory.

The word "choice" implies having several different options... And each alternative might be attractive in its own right, but also uniquely risky.

The Doors to My Future

You're standing in a long hallway full of doors. Behind each door is a different career and, consequently, a different life. Before reaching for any particular handle, ask yourself:

What will I have to leave at this door?
Along with muddy shoes, what else will you have to part ways with? This question is about the sacrifices you'll have to make, such as cutting back on certain activities, moving to another country, or jeopardizing certain relationships.

What will I bring with me?

What resources are you carrying inside? Your hands might be full of skills and talents (which can also be developed as you go, by the way). You might also have a bag stuffed full of perseverance and determination, the support of loved ones, past experiences, and useful skills. Also, consider the funds needed for education and/or additional training in your chosen field.

What awaits me behind this door?

Once you open it, what opportunities, challenges, and potential threats will be facing you? And does this door lead to a mansion or apartment building, with many stops (intermediate steps) along the way to the room you're seeking—and, if so, what are they?

Door B	**Door C**	**Door D**
Profession	Profession	Profession
At this door, I'll leave	At this door, I'll leave	At this door, I'll leave
I'll bring	I'll bring	I'll bring
Behind this door is	Behind this door is	Behind this door is

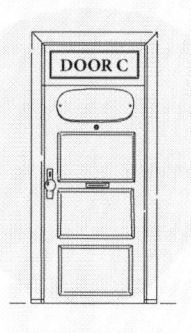

Remember the concept of tunnel vision? When choosing a profession, don't keep your gaze glued to just one spot—you risk missing every other path leading elsewhere.

If you pull and pull on your chosen door but it just won't budge, or if you open it and then decide to step back out, the remaining doors will remind you of other options. Moreover, at every stage of your journey, new doors will appear. But to spot them, you'll need to learn to look around.

To accurately assess potential threats and avoid being misled by false information, you'll need to use critical thinking and learn as much as possible about the profession you're interested in.

It most likely WON'T happen.

It might happen, or it might NOT.

It's most likely to happen.

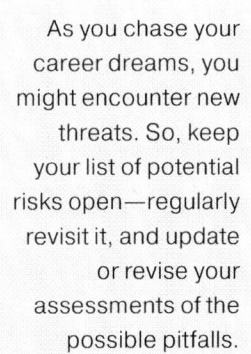

As you chase your career dreams, you might encounter new threats. So, keep your list of potential risks open—regularly revisit it, and update or revise your assessments of the possible pitfalls.

Is copying someone else's career choice a bad idea?

Not necessarily. You might choose the same path as someone else if you genuinely believe, with reasoning, that it's right for you. But if you're making a choice without thinking, simply imitating someone or blindly following tradition, you might end up with a future chosen by someone else rather than one you've picked out for yourself.

Danger Ahead!

As you already know, no strategy is complete without understanding potential threats, difficulties, and risks. This is especially true for choosing and pursuing a career. The job market, your place of residence, or other factors might change. For instance, a profession that seems promising and desirable now could be replaced by artificial intelligence in the future.

It's a good idea to anticipate potential threats for each career choice in advance.

For example:

Profession _____

I won't be able to get into a program specializing in this.

I'll lose interest in this profession.

In the future, this profession will stop being in demand.

It'll be hard to find a job in this field because of competition.

_____

_____

_____

_____

Any threat assessment is just an educated guess since we can't predict the future with absolute certainty. But for each potential threat, it's important to have a plan of action ready. If you do run into one of the anticipated threats, you'll already know how to handle it.

The End... Or Is It?

The modern world changes so rapidly that it's hard to say for certain what it will look like in a few years, much less in a couple of decades. So, worry not: The choices you make today are unlikely to be final and permanent.

This applies to choosing a profession as well. What seems like an ideal future goal today may turn out to be just a new beginning or a stepping stone to something else over time.

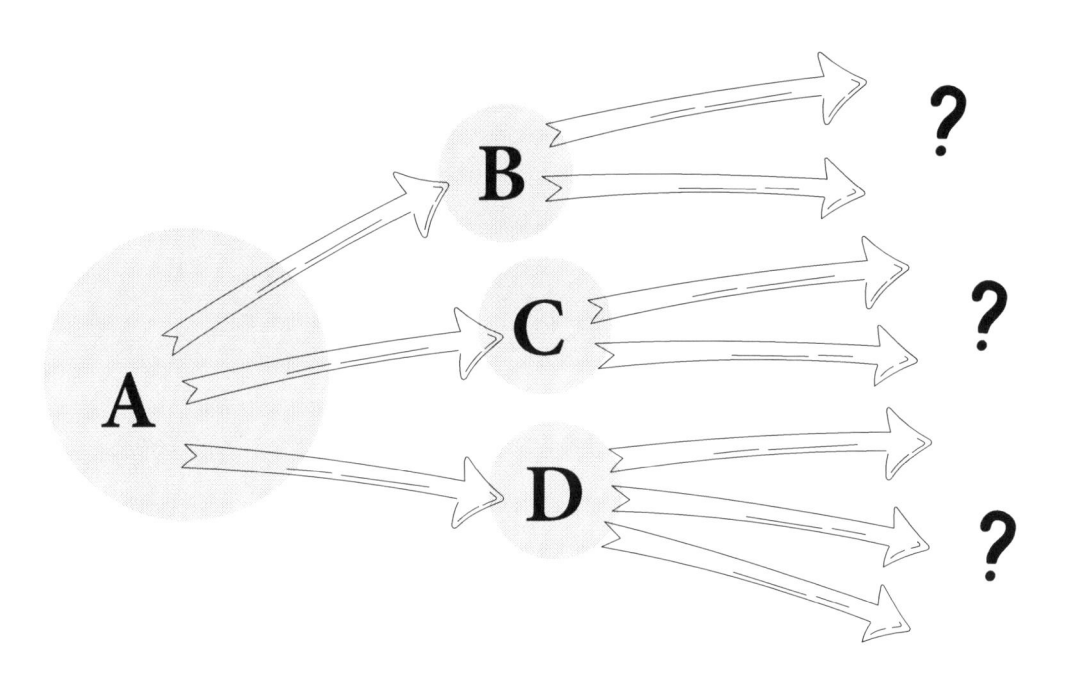

You can't expect a path as complex and exciting as a career path to be perfectly smooth and straight. Sometimes it will lead uphill, sometimes downhill. Sometimes you will hit a dead end, and sometimes arrive at a crossroads.

So now's a great time to ask yourself again what your process of choosing and pursuing a career looks like.

- ○ Like a steady, straight climb up a mountain.
- ○ Like a journey through the hills, with its peaks and valleys.
- ○ Like wandering through a forest full of winding paths and forks.
- ○ *Like a* _____

To avoid getting lost, regularly ask yourself: "Where am I now?", "Which door brought me here?", "Where am I headed and where do I want to end up?"

Basically...

Strategic thinking helps you:

- [ ] Identify initial opportunities when choosing a career.
- [ ] Consider how the present and future can be connected.
- [ ] Think about several career options.
- [ ] Analyze and evaluate each option.
- [ ] Understand that career choice doesn't have to be a one-time, irreversible decision.
- [ ] Not fear making mistakes and experimenting on your career selection journey.

HOW STRATEGIC THINKING HELPS YOU LEARN AND GROW

Are you stuck in class or slogging through a boring textbook at home, wondering why you're doing it? Do you think half of your lessons are just a waste of time?

○ Ugh, exactly!
○ Only sometimes.
○ No, never.
○ Or _____

In the "here and now," we're often driven by momentary interests and moods, and our current successes or failures. This can affect how we engage with our studies—either helping us focus and absorb information or, conversely, reducing our enthusiasm and interest in what we're learning.

"Today we covered evolutionary theory. Yesterday it was Ancient Greek history. Tomorrow we're memorizing new theorems. I don't even see why I need to learn this stuff at all!" (Elliot, 15 years old)

A good strategy helps overcome the short-term perspective on what you're doing and turns studying into a process of achieving clear strategic goals. This time travel into the future isn't always easy or exciting, but with strategic thinking, it becomes meaningful and productive.

You're Welcome, Future Me!

To start, it's helpful to understand the value of what you're learning. This value is determined less by immediate interest and emotions and more by a thoughtful perspective from the future, at varying degrees of temporal distance.

Write down what you are currently studying (for example, this week at school, university, extracurricular activities, additional courses, or independently). Be specific about the topics, knowledge, and skills you are getting the hang of.

Speaking skills in a foreign language.

🕐 will be useful in the near future,

📅 might be useful in about a year,

∞ could come in handy in _____ *years,*

⊖ probably won't be useful at all.

> Flip back to the previous section— what knowledge and skills might be useful to you, taking into account the professions your heart is set on?

> Are there completely useless pieces of knowledge and skills that will NEVER EVER be useful?

"I think I need English right now to talk to people from all over the world and watch shows in their original language. In a year, I'll be choosing where to continue my education. I'm interested in biology and math; knowing the lingo of these topics will definitely come in handy for college applications. As for a few years down the road... Hmm, hard to say. It'd be great to understand ecology, geography, and history in English so I can talk about various topics and be seen as a well-rounded person." (Sven, 15)

Where and How

Choose something from the previous list and think more deeply about **where** and **how** it might be useful.

🕐 In the near future, I will need to know or be able to

_____

_____

This will be useful for _____

_____

In order to _____

_____

📅 In about a year, I will need to know or be able to

_____

_____

This will be useful for _____

_____

In order to _____

_____

∞ In _____ years, I will need to know or be able to

_____

_____

This will be useful for _____

_____

In order to _____

_____

Now you have a clearer idea of where to focus your efforts during your studies. And most importantly, you understand why.

Are there any knowledge and skills that you will need in the future but that you're not currently learning or acquiring?

My Learning Strategy

Now we can move on to your strategy for learning and growth. The first step? Understanding what results you're trying to get by mastering one topic or another.

What can be considered a learning outcome?

- [ ] What I'll come to know in a certain subject or field.
- [ ] What I'll get really good at doing and which skills I'll develop.
- [ ] What I'll understand deeply and thoroughly.
- [ ] How much money I'll be earning after getting my education.

Learning outcomes are the changes that happen within you as you study and grow. Your knowledge, abilities, skills, capacities, and understanding can all evolve. How do they change? They deepen, expand, and improve.

You can think of it as growing a garden inside you, with roots reaching down farther and farther and new leaves sprouting up constantly.

For example, for a few years now I've been studying _____

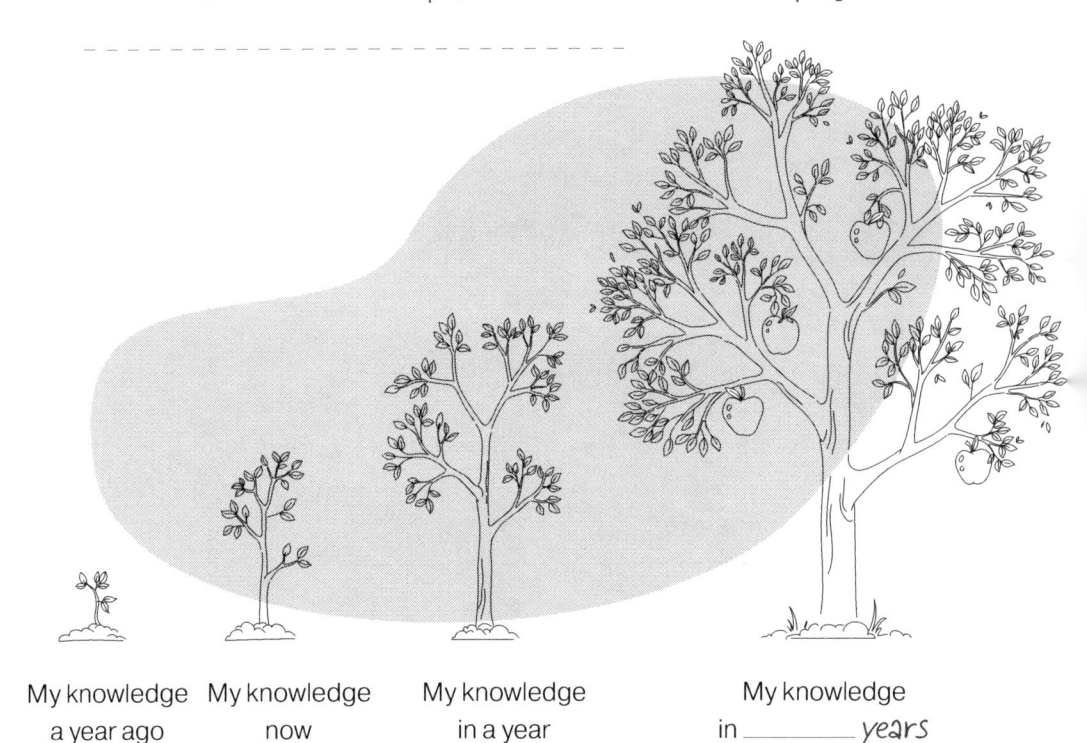

Learning outcomes are like the sun the stalks of your knowledge are constantly stretching towards. As for your future earnings, they'll just be the fruit of your labor—figuratively and, well, even more figuratively.

My knowledge a year ago   My knowledge now   My knowledge in a year   My knowledge in _____ *years*

What did you know about this a year ago? I'm sure you've really leveled up since then! And just imagine where you'll be in the future—a total pro, right? Go ahead, take a moment to daydream about how awesome your skills will be.

Turn Your Future Outcomes into Specific Goals

When you clearly define what you plan to know, be able to do, and understand as a result of your studies, you'll have your **learning objectives**. Try setting such goals for the upcoming year in one or more areas of knowledge.

In a year I'll know

In a year I'll be able to do

In a year I'll understand

In a year I'll master

You can plan your learning goals for two or five years out, but if you're just starting to think about them, begin with a one-year period.

Are good grades also a learning outcome?

To answer this, see if a grade fits into any of these categories: "I will know...", "I will be able to...", "I will understand...", or "I will master...". A grade really isn't the result, goal, or purpose of learning. Learning just for grades is like growing trees just to measure their height. We study to develop our qualities, knowledge, abilities, skills, and talents. A grade simply helps measure your academic progress and personal growth. And, if you think about it, is this measurement always accurate?

Identify Your Top Priorities for Learning and Development

You know who can be considered an expert from the section on critical thinking.

Even if you want to know everything about everything, let's be real—you can't absorb and process all the knowledge humanity has amassed. So, it's a good idea to choose a few areas that seem most important to you and focus on defining the subjects you want to grow in.

In some areas, you can dive **deep**—farther and farther into a particular trench until you become a true expert.

In others, you can expand **broadly**—gaining lots of general knowledge and widening your horizons drastically.

Choosing between these options is also a key part of your learning and development strategy.

I aim to have (broad) knowledge of areas such as

_____

_____

_____

I strive to have a (deep) understanding and be an expert in

_____

_____

_____

A person who combines broad knowledge across various fields with deep expertise and skills in one specific area is called a T-shaped individual.

A person who is deeply knowledgeable in one specific area but lacks a broad perspective in others is called an I-shaped individual. Where do you think this name originates from?

> **Can you have deep knowledge in more than one field?**
>
> Absolutely, if you have the interest and resources to dive deeply into different, and sometimes unrelated, areas—like a programmer who absolutely owns recreational soccer games on the weekends, or a biologist who sells her Van Gogh-level paintings. Typically, we study deeply in areas that are important for our chosen profession. The rest is for enjoyment, curiosity, and expanding our general knowledge.

Determine What Resources You Need to Get There

For effective learning and achieving goals, you'll need resources. These can be **external**—related to your environment and learning tools—or **internal**—such as your time, energy, and willpower.

Try estimating the resources needed to achieve one of your learning objectives:

My learning objective: In a year, I will

- -

To achieve this goal, I need:

External resources:

- Time dedicated to studying the subject or topic. ☐
- Information and reliable study materials. ☐
- A teacher or tutor who helps me learn more effectively. ☐
- Funds to cover additional expenses (paid courses, sessions, textbooks). ☐
- Support from loved ones in my pursuit of this goal. ☐
- And also ☐

- -
- -

Internal resources:

- Lots of enthusiasm and interest in studying this topic or subject. ☐
- A strong work ethic (how long I can work on study materials without throwing in the towel). ☐
- Skills in effective time management for studying. ☐
- Initial ability to understand and retain new material.
- And also ☐

- -
- -

▨ I have enough of this resource
◸ This resource is available, but limited
☐ This resource is not available
☒ I don't need this resource

Analyzing resources is essential to assess how achievable your learning goals are.

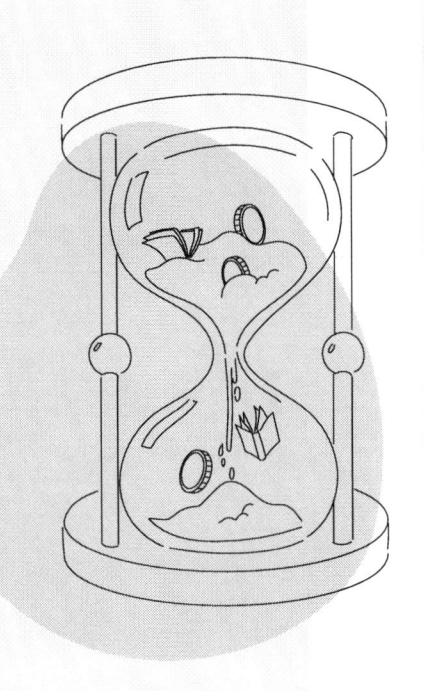

Uh-oh, I don't have enough resources...

If **external resources** are lacking, it's worth investing more time in finding them. For instance, there are countless scholarships available to make education more affordable. You can also explore alternatives: instead of a summer language school, look for a free online language exchange club.

If **internal resources** are lacking, consider whether you can find or develop them for an important goal. It's possible that some of your resources are being spent on less important things—like mind-numbing scrolling on social media. Sometimes, there really aren't enough resources available. In these cases, you might need to adjust your goal—either by scaling it down or postponing it to a future date to allow time to gather what you need.

Create a Plan for Achieving Your Learning Goals

You know what they say: If you fail to make your strategy into a plan, you plan to fail. Or something like that. In any case, a plan turns our ideas and goals into concrete actions and results.

You already know what you want to focus on in the near future, in a year, or even several years from now. You understand which areas you aim to delve deeply into and which ones you want to broaden.

All that's left is to specify the timeline, and your **strategic plan** will be ready. It might look like this:

MONTH	20___ yr.	20___ yr.	20___ yr.
January	I'll know		
February			I'll be able to
March			
April	I'll be able to		
May			
June			
July		I'll be able to	
August			
September			
October		I'll master	
November			
December			

Keep this plan handy to refer to and manage your time effectively across different days and weeks. Let it be your roadmap for navigating through new knowledge and skills.

A **strategic plan** is a long-term plan that outlines only the major goals. From this, shorter plans are typically created for the month or week.

When setting approximate timelines for achieving different goals, take your resources and daily workload into account.

To learn effectively, remember more, and organize knowledge better, check out the sections on systematic and creative thinking.

You can write down your plan at the end of this workbook.

A strategic plan should guide you without confining you. Feel free to make adjustments as your priorities, goals, conditions, and resources change. The most important part isn't to meet every deadline, but to understand what you are striving for. This plan helps you view yourself and your development from a future perspective.

Can I only study things that will be useful in the future?

We don't study solely to apply our knowledge practically. Learning is a fundamental part of being human. Discovering new things brings pleasure (our brain releases the happiness hormone, dopamine, when we learn something new), energizes us, and boosts our confidence. Interested in art even if you don't plan to make it your career? Passionate about cars but not aiming to be a mechanic? Simply enjoy exploring what inspires you!

Let's Review

Strategic thinking helps:

- [ ] Better understand why you learn and study.
- [ ] Reflect on which knowledge and skills will be useful in the future.
- [ ] Set clear goals for your learning and development.
- [ ] Identify areas for your growth.
- [ ] Plan how to achieve your strategic goals.
- [ ] View each day of studying from a future perspective.
- [ ] Find time not just for useful knowledge but also for enjoyable learning experiences.

I THINK OUTSIDE THE BOX

I solve problems, make discoveries, and invent new things—all the while being creative and having fun!

What can I surprise people with and how?

Can I think about this differently?

Who said I couldn't do it this way?

How can I become more original?

Where do awesome ideas come from?

Am I creative enough for this?

What if...

WHAT IS CREATIVE THINKING AND WHY DO YOU NEED IT?

When you face a problem, task, or tough decision, it might seem like there are one or a few correct, conventional solutions—you just need to find them. That's how standard thinking works. But what happens when creative thinking comes into play?

A Creative Thinking Experiment

You have four shapes labeled F, L, E, and X.

Three of them share a common feature, but one is an imposter and doesn't belong. Can you figure out which is the odd one out?

What are your initial instincts telling you?

The odd one out is _____,
because _____
_____

Usually, the ideas and solutions that come to mind first aren't the most creative. But there are exceptions.

F ▪ L ◯ E ▲ X ★

In fact, this task can have multiple solutions. Any of the shapes could be considered to not fit. Try to find as many solutions as possible and evaluate each one as either conventional or unconventional (original).

The odd one out could be...

F, because _____

L, because _____

E, because _____

X, because _____

__, because _____

__, because _____

__, because _____

Standard solutions are based on clear rules (like the rules of geometry or logic).

Unconventional solutions break away from the usual rules and patterns. These kinds of solutions often surprise us.

What if you add something extra to the shapes? What if you turn them upside down?

What if...?

FLEX

You might have caught on by now that this isn't just a random arrangement of letters...

We chose to call the shapes by these letters because creative thinking is the most flexible of all! It breaks the usual rules and says, "Don't be afraid to experiment. Forget the restrictions. Think it can't be done any other way? It can. It can also be done this way and that way too."

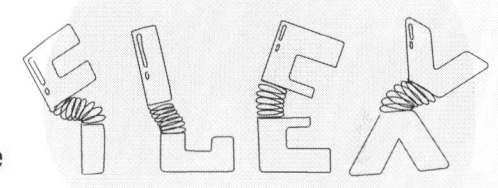

The flexibility of creative thinking allows us to generate multiple ideas and solutions for the same problem. Creative thinking also thrives on novelty and originality. This is what enables us to come up with completely new and unconventional ideas.

Did you feel the power of creative thinking while solving the shape puzzle?

○ Yes, I came up with a lot of ideas.
○ Some of my ideas were new.
○ A few of my ideas were original and unconventional.

It's not always easy to switch on creative thinking quickly, especially if your school, family, or work environments don't really encourage non-traditional ideas and solutions. But even in those cases, you can still learn to think creatively! By the way, why should you?

To test the **novelty** of your ideas, ask your friends or family to solve the same puzzle. Compare their ideas with yours. If no one came up with the solution you thought of, then you can consider your idea truly original!

Well, what if we rephrased that question as "Why think inside the box?"

Why Think Outside the Box?

"I decided to throw a house party for my friends for my birthday. I wanted to totally wow them with something they'd never expect. I only had my allowance to spend. So, here's what I came up with... (Polly, 15 years old)

What could Polly have come up with?

Get this, Polly also surprised her friends with dishes made from real fried insects! Thanks to her creativity, her guests were gasping, laughing, and having a great time the whole night.

◯ I could come up with something even more creative!
◯ Wow, the guests must have been impressed.
◯ Or _____

Creative thinking isn't just for surprising people and having fun. Where else could a creative perspective and unconventional approach come in handy?

When I'm...

Choosing what to dress as for Halloween. ☐

Looking to give my friend a truly unique gift. ☐

Brainstorming ways to make my blog stand out. ☐

Trying to grab my peers' attention on environmental issues. ☐

Working on a presentation. ☐

Tackling a tough level in a strategic game. ☐

Brainstorming ideas for my startup. ☐

_____ ☐

_____ ☐

_____ ☐

_____ ☐

_____ ☐

_____ ☐

You can, of course, mark the boxes with the usual check marks or Xs. But you could also think of a symbol no one has ever used before!

Creativity can be infused into just about anything. And when it comes to unusual problems, they simply can't be solved using typical solutions. So let's get to flexing that creativity muscle!

Isn't creativity just for painters and writers?

Creativity and art are not the same thing. With creative thinking, people can generate new ideas and solve problems in any area of life, regardless of whether it's tidying up the house or building rockets. Whether you need creativity if you're not a painter or a writer is up to you to decide.

CHECK MARKS AND XS!?

NOT AGAIN!

SPRUCE THIS PAGE UP A LITTLE...

In a Nutshell

Creative thinking is the ability to...

Think flexibly and unconventionally.

Come up with many ideas and solutions for one problem.

Generate new and original thoughts.

Surprise others with your ideas.

Flawlessly follow rules and instructions.

Always seek just one solution for a problem.

Think within strict boundaries.

Act the way you're expected to and never try new approaches.

CAN I BECOME MORE CREATIVE? ABSOLUTELY

Like anything else, creativity is a skill that can be improved throughout your life. So anyone can become more creative. And you especially, because right now we're going to work on your creativity!

What's My Baseline?

But before jumping too far ahead, let's get a feel for how creative you are right now. Turn the page, read every scenario, and imagine how you would act.

Circle every option that you would be okay with. For each scenario, you can select as many options as you like:

- I won't be intimidated by the task and problem at hand.
- I'll experiment and look at the situation from different angles.
- I'll make up as many ideas as I can.
- I'll try to come up with something that's never been done before.
- I'll try to think of something unusual and original.

When you mark one or another option, envision exactly what you would do in that situation and how.

You got an invite to a birthday party... two hours before it starts. So you don't have a gift, and all the stores are closed. And you've already scoured your couch for loose change without any luck.

Your teacher assigned you to pitch a proposal for convincing people to reduce their water usage. You have a week to complete it.

Your bike just got a flat tire while you're out in the countryside. There's no public transport, you don't have any tools, and the thought of walking all the way back? Not exactly appealing.

Any difficult problem or challenge is no match for a creative thinker! In their eyes, tough moments are invitations to grow and show their stuff!

A friend asked for help rearranging furniture. The challenge: How to create more free space without removing anything from the room.

You've been asked to manage the company's social media at your new job, but no one has a clue what to post or, well, how to post it.

You've been accepted into a young entrepreneurs program, where you're given $1,000 with the catch that it must be invested in your very own business idea.

Likewise, creative thinkers don't shy away from expressing their wildest, wackiest ideas, even if nobody else ends up getting it.

A recent problem or task you had to tackle:

_____

_____

_____

_____

For each marked square, you get one creativity point. The more points, the more creative you are... Pretty straight-forward. Is there a limit to creativity? Of course not!

Where Does Creativity Start?

Nope, not with generating ideas. It begins with the ability to notice the unusual around you and draw inspiration from it. What do you find creative?

The most creative place in my city is

_____

because _____

The most creative place in my school is

_____

because _____

The most creative room among my friends belongs to

_____

because _____

The most creative café I've ever been to is

_____

because _____

The most creative thing I've ever bought is

_____

because _____

The most creative person I know is

_____

because _____

When we learn by watching what other people do and then replicating them, including but not limited to how to be creative thinkers, it's called "**observational learning**."

The more you notice new and unconventional things, events, and people around you, the more your brain adapts to the unusual, gets inspired, and starts coming up with creative ideas on its own.

Is imitation really the highest form of flattery?

When you marvel at someone's original idea and it pushes you to create something bold and unique of your own—that's inspiration at work. But if you simply copy someone's idea and claim it as your own, that's more like stealing ideas than being creative.

A Different Perspective

You can spot something new even in an ordinary object just by changing your point of view. Creative thinking is also about the ability to see things, events, tasks, and problems from fresh and unexpected angles.

Which way is the plane flying: towards you or away from you?

The answer depends on your perspective. If you look at the plane from below, it seems like it's flying:

And if you look from above, it seems like the plane is flying:

Try this experiment with a friend without giving them any hints on how to look at the drawing. See how many people use different perspectives and provide multiple answers.

This exercise isn't just for looking at silly pictures—you can view life situations and problems from different angles, too! From one perspective, it might seem like opportunities are flying away from you. But from another angle, you might see that they are swiftly approaching!

139

Abracadabra!
The Art of Transformation

The art of transforming one idea into another is a skill unique to creative thinking. That's how it gives birth to new and original solutions.

Go ahead—try turning this fly into an elephant!

Who knows, maybe that fly was one of the snacks at Polly's party! But could there have been an elephant too?

By the way, creative thinking thrives when your mind is in a «fluttering» mode, with your attention flitting around like a butterfly. That's why brainstorming new ideas is perfect during leisurely walks or long, scalding showers.

Are there ways to do that without even touching the drawing? And who said you need to use the drawing at all?

Try turning the word "fly" into "elephant" in just a few steps using a chain of associations. Each new word should be linked to the previous one in some way. For example, here's how you could transform "hawk" into "butterfly":

(hawk) — sky — sun — flower — (butterfly)

Your turn:

(hawk) -------------------- (butterfly)

The game of transforming the fly into an elephant hones your ability to use **associations** for generating new ideas. Associations are yet another powerful tool in the creative thinking toolbox.

Come up with pairs of words that would be a real head-scratcher to transform from one to the other. For example "jelly" and "astronaut." Write them down so you don't forget:

jelly   and   astronaut

_____   and   _____

_____   and   _____

_____   and   _____

You can also add a twist: make sure there are at least five but no more than 10 words in between. Or come up with your own rule! Don't be afraid to experiment and change up the game. Suggest playing it with friends or family—it'll be a blast!

What If...

What if we imagine that the creature on the left is a "flyphant"? Or an "elephly"? Or maybe a "trunk-wing"?

What kind of body parts would these mutants have? Keep drawing, redrawing, and tweaking your sketches to create something new every time!

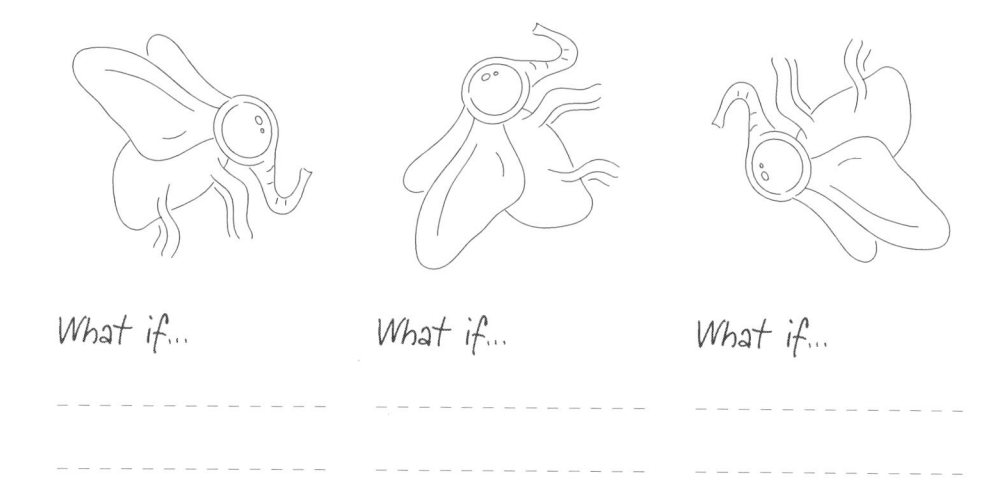

What if...   What if...   What if...

With creative thinking, you can imagine anything. Combine the incompatible. Mix and match the mismatched. And end up with something one of a kind.

But how do we use that to our benefit—and the world's? The answer is coming up in the next section.

Coming up with new rules for familiar games is a great way to exercise your creative thinking. Try inventing new rules for your favorite games—whether they're word games, board games, or video games. Or better yet, why not create... a whole new game?

The question "**What if…**" is another method of thinking creatively.

What if you flip each drawing upside down?

What if you imagine that all three drawings are parts of one larger picture?

What if you tear your gaze away from your phone while walking and look around?

What if you mentally transform colorful spots, lines, cracks, shapes, and holes into creatures

141

Now I'll work on my creative thinking by:

☐ Studying and strengthening my creativity.
☐ Noticing creativity around me and drawing inspiration from it.
☐ Stealing other people's ideas and claiming them as my own.
☐ Looking at the same thing from different angles.
☐ Transforming one idea into another.
☐ Using the power of associations.
☐ Combining dissimilar ideas, things, and details.
☐ Asking myself: "What if..."

HOW CREATIVITY HELPS YOU LEARN AND GROW

Creativity isn't just fun and games. Channeling your creativity is like suddenly being able to fly: it allows you to reach new heights in anything. Whether it's in studying, video games, or just your daily tasks, creativity can help you understand better, remember more, and invent new ideas, approaches, and solutions.

Don't Just Make Mistakes, Invent Them

How about deliberately learning from your mistakes? Try intentionally coming up with incorrect answers to questions and assignments from textbooks, books, or courses. But remember, each wrong answer should also be explainable.

What does 1 + 1 equal?

1 + 1 = 0 if these numbers represent a $1 debt between two people, effectively canceling each other out.

1 + 1 = 0 if it refers to an electron and a positron, which annihilate each other upon collision.

1 + 1 = _____

1 + 1 = _____

1 + 1 = _____

To be wrong on purpose, you first need to know the correct solution. Then, you can let your imagination run wild and twist the answer however you like! The more absurd, the better!

**Now let's kick it up a notch:
What happens to water at 0°C?**

In a world where all laws of physics work in reverse, water boils at 0°C.

Water _____

Water _____

Water _____

Water _____

Once you come up with enough incorrect answers, tell yourself: "It could be this way, and that way, and another way… But in reality, it's this way: [the correct answer]."

Use Associations

There's no better way to remember something than by linking it to what you already know. You can do this through associations—spontaneous connections between different ideas, things, or experiences.

"I just couldn't remember the value of π (pi). Then I realized that it sounds like "pie"! So, I imagined π as a pie divided into 3 slices, with 14 crumbs left over. After that, I've never forgotten that number! I'll probably still remember it on my deathbed."
(Micah, 14)

Utilize associations to memorize formulas, dates, laws, and names! These associations are like bridges connecting what you know or can imagine with what you need to remember.

What do you associate with the number π?

_____

_____

_____

_____

Transform

Remember how creative thinking has the power to turn one thing or idea into another? You can use this in your studies. For example, turn a snooze-fest of a text into a song or a drawing. Memorize a seemingly endless chain of world capitals by going on an imaginary journey. For instance, the molecular structure of water, H_2O, can be transformed into:

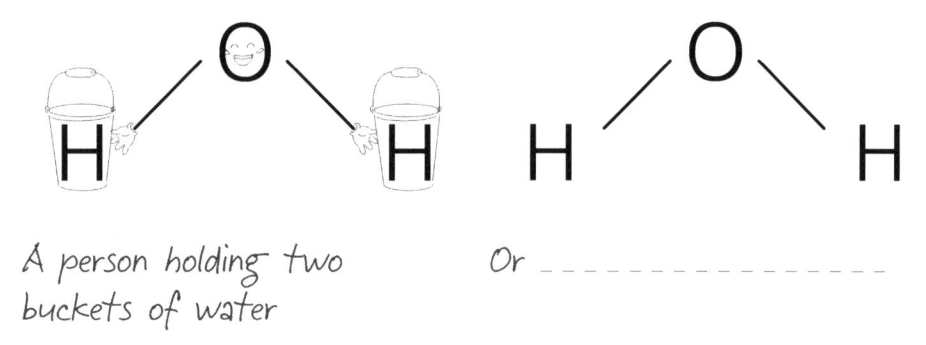

H—O—H   H—O—H

A person holding two buckets of water   Or _____

...And Be Transformed

Want to better understand and remember how something works? Imagine yourself as that object and study...your own self.

I am an internal combustion engine. Inside me, a series of controlled explosions make the pistons move up and down, turning the chemical energy of fuel into mechanical power.

I am a bacterium. My life is mostly about reproducing by splitting in two and absorbing nutrients from my environment. My biggest enemy? A virus named Bacteriophage (in our world, that name is forbidden to speak aloud).

I am _____

_____

_____

_____

You can transform into the characters or people you're studying, and think about their lives and achievements as if you're talking about yourself. Turn the page and give it a try!

"In biology class, we were learning about Charles Darwin's theory of evolution, and I didn't really get it at first. But then I imagined myself as Darwin, sailing around the world on the HMS Beagle. I'm exploring the Galápagos Islands, watching birds and tortoises, and noticing how little differences help them survive in different places. And then it hit me: species change and adapt over time to survive, and that's how evolution works!" (Karim, 15 years old)

Try it yourself:

I'm Albert Einstein. I came up with the theory of relativity.

I'm Frida Kahlo, the most famous Mexican artist in the world

I'm the whale from Herman Melville's Moby Dick.

I'm Scout Finch from To Kill a Mockingbird.

I'm _____

I'm _____

I'm _____

Ask "What If..."

Don't forget the ultimate question of creative thinking. No matter what you're studying, this question can bring even the dullest topic to life and push the boundaries of what's possible.

What if our planet was square?

What if humans had gills?

What if Alexander the Great had conquered India?

What if the internet existed 200 years ago?

What if dinosaurs never went extinct?

What if there were no commas in any language?

What if _____

What if _____

What if _____

What if _____

What if _____

When you're pondering these questions, bring in your friends, family, and teachers. If someone brushes it off or thinks it's silly, don't get discouraged. Not everyone knows how to tap into their creative thinking.

It's not just about asking these questions—it's about diving into them and coming up with the craziest answers and stories you can imagine.

Combine and Invent

Need to come up with a topic for a school project? Or develop a startup idea for business school? Try using the creative thinking tool called the "idea builder."

"I want to enter an essay contest about how modern technology affects people and the world around us. I really want to come up with an interesting and original topic..." (Zach, 15)

To use the idea builder, start by framing a few key questions—these will be your foundation. For example: What technologies? What do they affect? How do they affect it? The answers to these questions are the building blocks you'll use to construct your topic.

Filling out the table on a separate sheet, you can cut it into the different sections and then combine any of them with each other to see what ideas emerge.

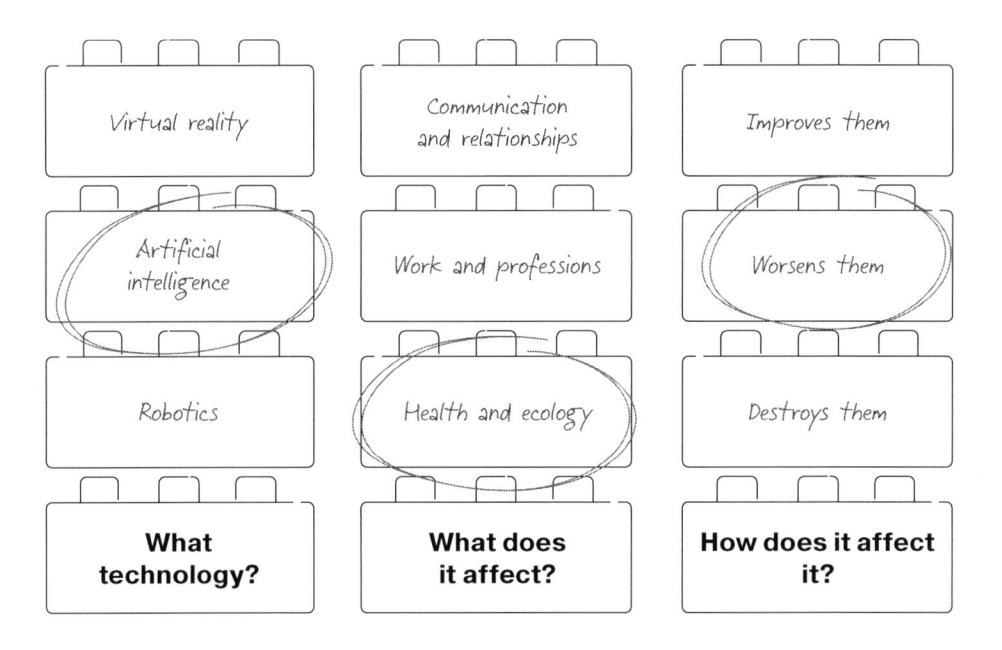

What technology?	What does it affect?	How does it affect it?
Virtual reality	Communication and relationships	Improves them
Artificial intelligence	Work and professions	Worsens them
Robotics	Health and ecology	Destroys them

Now you can mentally combine any of these blocks together and see what comes out. For example:

Artificial intelligence
+
Health and ecology
+
Worsens them

And you have a ready-made essay topic:
"How AI Worsens Human Health and the Environment."

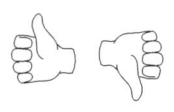

You can use the idea builder for more than just academic projects. It's great for brainstorming any kind of idea: organizing a party, finding the perfect gift for a friend... or even creating your own startup!

If the topic isn't quite right or seems unoriginal, keep experimenting. Mix and match different numbers of blocks, not just three. Or come up with new questions and add more columns to your idea builder. Challenge your friends to see who can come up with the most themes and the most original ones.

All our ideas:

150

Startup Builder

Try filling it out completely and writing as many ideas as you can by mixing and matching different elements.

Start filling in the sections from the bottom up, stacking them like building blocks. If you run out of space, just add more blocks on top!

What can I do?	What are my talents?	Who can I do this for?	Where can I do it?	Who can I do this with?	Who will pay for this?
Creating	Coding				
Selling	Persuading				
Managing	Drawing				
Fixing					

You can draw the blocks on a separate sheet, cut them out, and sort them into 6 piles, mixing up each one. Then, blindly pick one block from each pile and come up with a business idea based on the combination. It's a great game for a group!

Feel free to swap out the building blocks of your idea generator and even change the main questions. Don't be afraid to play around with it—there's no such thing as a wrong answer. You're the one who decides what's exciting and achievable, no matter how outrageous your ideas might seem to everyone else.

My business ideas:

- -
- -
- -
- -
- -
- -

How will you use creative thinking for your learning and personal growth?

- [ ] I'll come up with wrong answers and compare them with the right ones.
- [ ] I'll use associations to remember important information.
- [ ] I'll turn what I'm studying into something fun and easy to remember.
- [ ] I'll imagine myself as the objects, animals, or people I'm learning about.
- [ ] I'll ask "What if…?" about everything I study.
- [ ] I'll experiment and invent using an idea generator.

UNCONVENTIONAL APPROACHES TO PROBLEM SOLVING

Problems… issues… troubles… If it's not one thing, it's another! Sometimes, it feels like there's no way out—like you're standing at the edge of a cliff, and every step you take just speeds up the fall. Creative thinking helps you see even the toughest problems from a fresh perspective.

How We View Our Problems

What do you see in this drawing?

_____

_____

Remember the airplane drawing from one of the previous sections? Try changing your perspective and imagine the drawing on this page differently. To do this, turn it upside down or use a mirror (but first, try flipping it mentally!).

What do you see now?

_____

_____

If we're inclined to view a problem as a tragedy, that's exactly how it will appear to us. Likewise, when you look at a drawing, you see what you were primed to see.

Were you able to imagine the drawing the other way before turning it upside down?

◯ Yes, I saw the second version immediately.
◯ I had an inkling that it could be flipped.
◯ No, that was a totally unexpected twist.

"At first, I saw someone falling into a pit. But now I see them climbing up a mountain. Every setback is just a lesson leading to something new." (Dani, 16)

A Different Perspective

Sometimes all it takes to rethink our problems is looking at them from a different angle or perspective.

"I used to feel really awkward giving presentations in front of the whole class. I felt like I was under a spotlight, and everyone was just staring at me. But then I talked to my teacher about it, and they told me to flip the script. Instead of just seeing myself up there, they said to imagine the class performing for me—some are playing the part of good listeners, others are cast as bullies, and some have the role of critics. And each of them also wants their part to be convincing and worthy of a standing ovation. Once I thought about it like that, it was way easier!" (Veronica, 15)

Even if someone insists that a problem is unsolvable and tries to get you down in the dumps, don't be quick to agree! Try flipping your problem on its head instead.

Try looking at one of your problems from different angles.

Describe how this problem looks to you:

_____

_____

_____

_____

_____

Look at the problem through the eyes of others.
What would they think about this problem?

The richest person on the planet _____

_____

The poorest person on the planet _____

_____

The wisest person on the planet _____

_____

The dumbest person on the planet _____

_____

Or _____

_____

Or _____

_____

Or _____

_____

Creative thinking is also the ability to look at things, events, tasks, and problems from new and unusual perspectives.

Now, mentally travel into the future and look at your problem as if time has passed. What will you think of this problem in:

10 years? _____
_____
_____
_____

20 years? _____
_____
_____
_____

___ years? _____
_____
_____
_____

And lastly, try looking at your problem the way aliens peering down at you from a UFO might see it. Ask yourself:

Is this problem big enough to be seen from space?

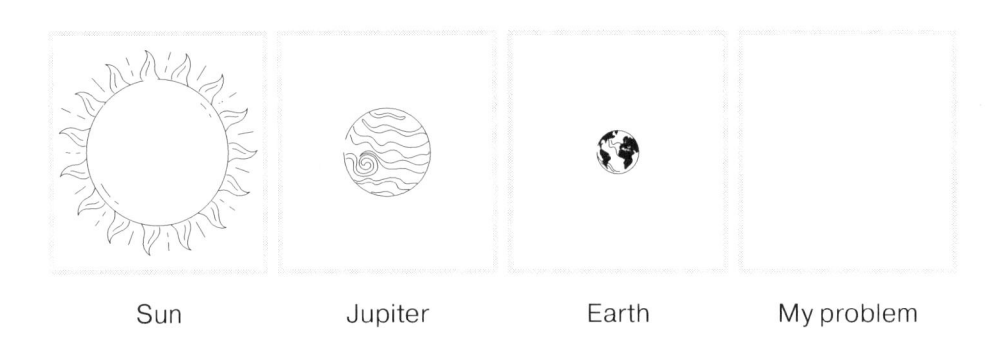

| Sun | Jupiter | Earth | My problem |

Is this problem as serious as other problems in the world?

○ There are bigger problems out there.
○ To me, it's the worst problem ever!

What's the worst that could happen if you don't solve this problem?

Imagine all the possible outcomes—even the most outlandish and far-fetched ones!

_____
_____
_____
_____
_____
_____
_____

"Yesterday, I washed my hair and was about to head out, but I glanced in the mirror and saw that it was a total disaster. I instantly stopped feeling like going out. But then I thought, 'What's really going to change in my life if I go outside with this mess on my head? Probably nothing major.' But just to be safe, I put on a cap anyway." (Jasper, 16 years old)

Did you manage to see something new in your problem or change how you think about it?

◯ It's really not as big of a deal as I thought.

◯ Now I understand better what I'm dealing with.

◯ It's still a problem.

◯ Or _____

Brainstorming Time!

If your problem still feels like a problem, it's time to tackle it. Creative thinking has your back with a classic method: brainstorming. The rules are simple: shut down your inner critic and fire up your idea generator.

1. Grab a sheet of paper and cut it into cards or use sticky notes. Prepare at least 10 main cards and about 10 spare ones.

2. Write down one idea or solution on each card. Don't judge the ideas as good, bad, or impossible—just write them down, no matter how weird they seem.

3. Make sure you've squeezed out every last drop of your creative juices. But don't rush to stop—more ideas might pop into your mind if you wait longer.

4. Once you've written down all your ideas, gather the cards together. Try to sort them into groups with similar ideas.

5. Pick one card from each stack and think over the ideas. Now, turn on your inner critic and ask yourself:

   - Can this idea actually work?
   - If not, why? What makes it hard to realize?
   - If yes, how will it solve my problem?
   - What are the upsides?
   - What are the downsides?
   - Can I tweak or improve this idea somehow?

Jot down any notes on the back of the cards and make sure to record any new ideas, even if they seem impossible!

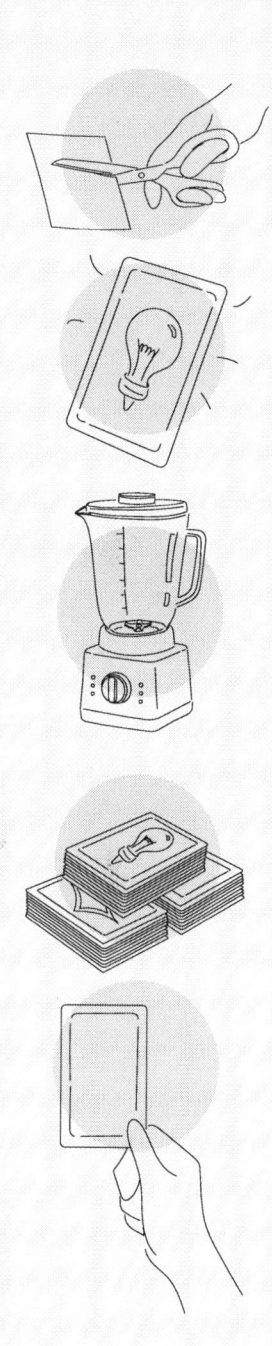

Shuffle through your cards, considering each one. The goal here isn't to find a quick fix but to engage in the process of deep thinking.

Show the ideas you've collected to a loved one. Invite them to brainstorm with you.

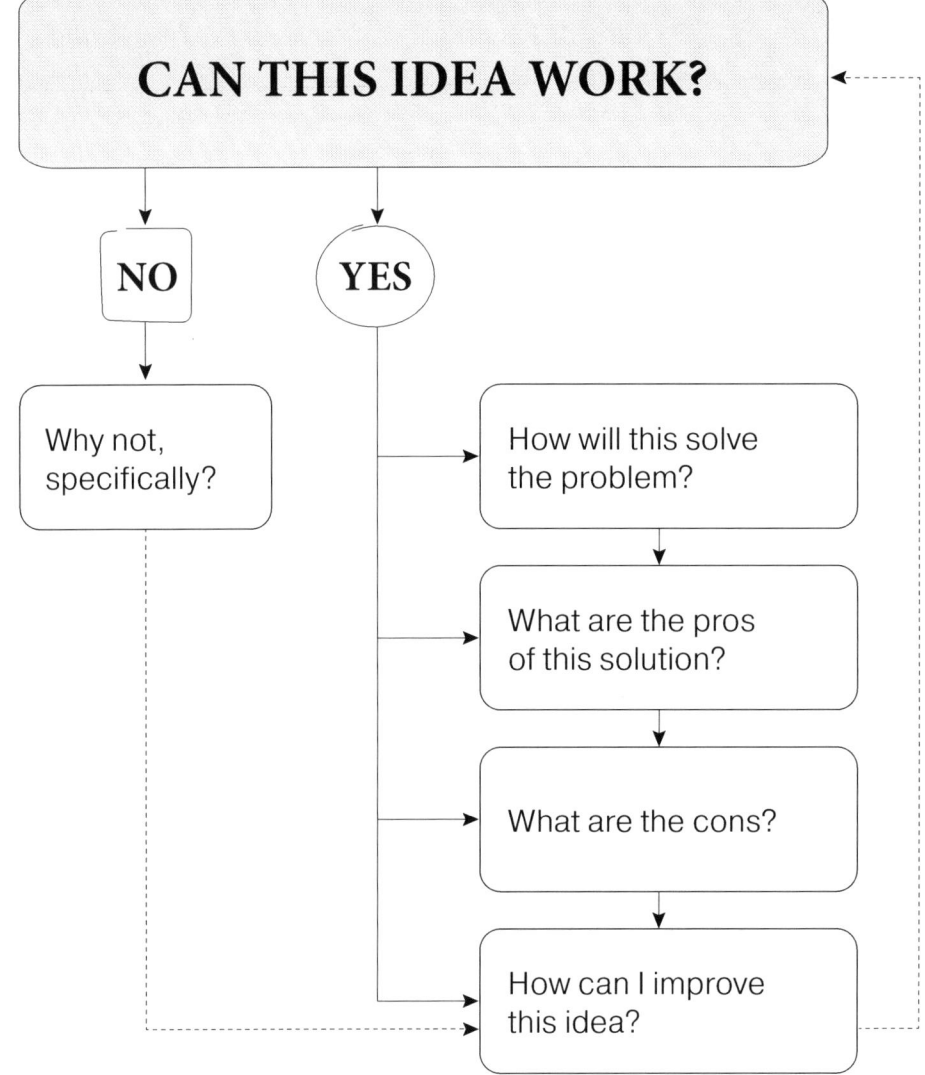

CAN THIS IDEA WORK?

- **NO** → Why not, specifically?
- **YES** →
  - How will this solve the problem?
  - What are the pros of this solution?
  - What are the cons?
  - How can I improve this idea?

Will this really help?

Sometimes solutions don't come while you're actively thinking about them. Instead, they appear later, when your mind has shifted to something else entirely. Creative thinking keeps working behind the scenes, mulling over different ideas in your subconscious (this is called "idea incubation" in science). It can spark a new idea at the most unexpected moment, so just give it time.

What I will do with my problem:

☐ I'll look at it from different angles and perspectives.

☐ I'll try to come up with as many ideas and solutions as possible.

☐ I won't limit myself to finding only the best of perfect solutions.

☐ I'll think through every solution, even if it doesn't seem to fit at first.

☐ I'll discuss the collected ideas with someone close to me.

☐ I'll be patient and give my mind time to come up with new ideas.

How do I bring order to my life?

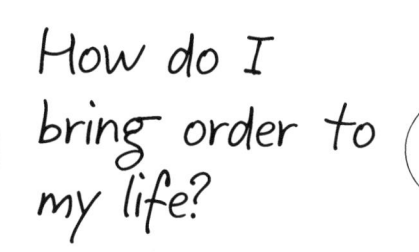

What affects my behavior?

I THINK ABOUT EVERYTHING SIMULTANEOUSLY
I keep things organized both around and within me, memorize information, and make decisions using systematic thinking

How are my actions connected?

To act or not to act?

How can I remember everything without getting it mixed up?

Can I make the wrong choices?

What might happen if I do this?

Why do I sometimes struggle with decision-making?

IS MY LIFE A SYSTEM?

Open your closet right now.

What do you see in there?

○ Neatly-folded clothes in straight stacks and a spotless floor.

○ What looks like the fallout from some sort of natural disaster.

○ Something in between.

Now imagine that your head is that closet. Except it doesn't contain lonely, single socks and old Halloween costumes you'll never wear again.

Instead, it's full of your…

Thoughts
Goals
Wishes
Problems
Feelings

What else?

Everything stored in your head is part of your inner world. And sometimes, just like a closet, it can get messy.

Now tell me:
Does the inside of your head look like the inside of your closet?

◯ Unlike my closet, my head is organized.
◯ Unlike my closet, my head is a total mess.
◯ Everything is neat in both my head and my closet.
◯ It's all chaos in both my head and my closet.
◯ Or

To get things in order—whether it's your closet, your head, or your life—you need a special kind of thinking. You'll learn about it soon.

But Why Is Order so Important?

Because—wait, I almost forgot about this section's experiment!

What do you see in this picture?

As soon as you run out of ideas, flip the page!

Do you see anything new in the picture? When elements are organized, they form a system, and something new appears from them—this is called **emergence** in science.

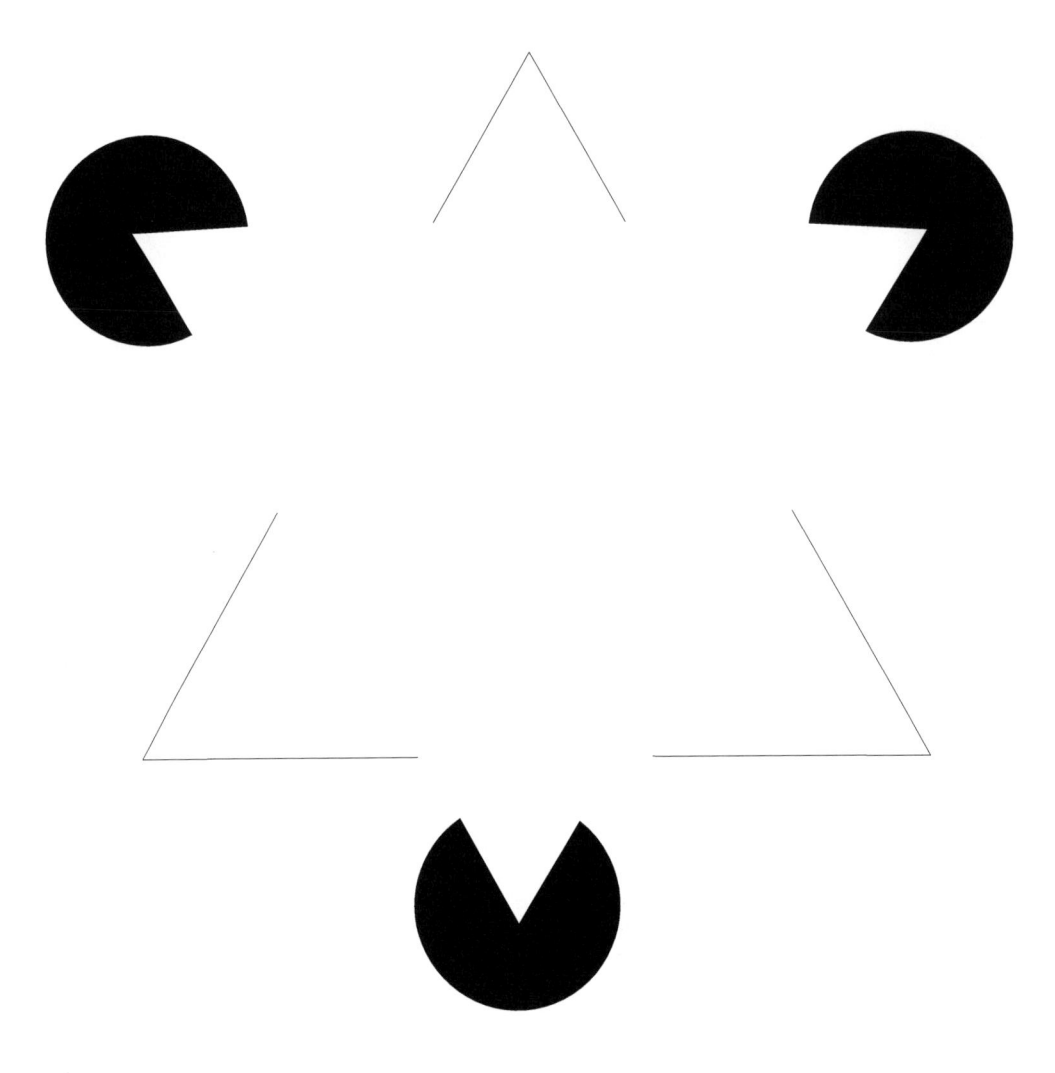

When is it easier to find what you need in your closet: when everything is spick and span or when it's like a tornado went through? And what about finding solutions to your problems: when your mind is tidy or when it's all over the place?

All the pieces are exactly the same, but something's different. What is it?

Write down your thoughts about this:

_ _

_ _

_ _

_ _

_ _

When you organize things and turn scattered details into a system, you start noticing what you didn't before—or something entirely new emerges.

By bringing order to different aspects of life, we see the root causes of our problems more clearly, find solutions faster, and make surprising discoveries. That's why order matters.

"I kept forgetting my keys at home and it was really frustrating. At some point, I got curious about why this was happening. I decided to figure it out by thinking through my morning routine, what I take with me, and my habits. That's when I realized I'm always texting while heading out the door, so I never notice the keys hanging right next to it."
(Mariana, 15 years old)

"I get a small allowance each month. I used to always run out of it and couldn't figure out where it was going. So, I decided to take control and started tracking my expenses. After a couple of weeks, I discovered that most of my money was going to soda, which I buy almost every day after school. And why didn't I notice how much I was spending on this before?"
(David, 16 years old)

Mariana and David decided to piece together the scattered details into a complete picture. Because of this, each of them recognized something new about their problem.

Order is a Mini-System

Getting your life and mind completely organized once and for all is a tall order, even for adults. It's way easier to make small adjustments and tidy up different aspects of your life and inner world bit by bit.

Where have you already managed to get things in order?

☐ In understanding which information I can trust.
☐ In my thoughts and wishes about my future career.
☐ In my ideas about job searching.
☐ _____
☐ _____
☐ _____
☐ _____
☐ _____

When you first get things in order, it might feel a bit shaky. Whether it's a new system for storing things, your outlook, your goals, or your spending, it can easily fall apart under the pressure of old habits and unexpected situations.

So, don't forget to revisit the earlier parts of the book and bring order back into your life. In this chapter, you'll discover what systemic thinking is and how to use its superpower to the fullest!

And finally, get your closet, desk, and backpack in order. Order around you leads to order within you.

WHAT IS SYSTEMATIC THINKING AND WHY DO YOU NEED IT?

Systemic thinking doesn't just help you get organized—it helps you understand something bigger. What is that something? Check out this picture. Imagine Gear 1 starts spinning clockwise. Where do you think Gear 2 will turn?

Point it out on the drawing with an arrow.

To solve this problem correctly, you need to answer two questions: How are all the parts **connected**? And how can one part **influence** the others?

Add as many new details to this system as you like. Conduct a super-complex mental experiment!

Try to figure out which directions the other gears will turn if the first one keeps spinning clockwise.

You can mentally experiment with this almost endlessly. For example, stop the mechanism and restart it, beginning with any gear. Imagine turning one gear in a different direction and see how the movement of the others changes. This is all thanks to systemic thinking!

What's the difference between systemic and strategic thinking?

Strategic thinking is the ability to view the present through a future lens, set goals, and plan how to achieve them. **Systemic thinking** is the ability to understand how different parts and aspects of your life affect each other and fit into the big picture. The best results come when these two superpowers work together!

Is Systemic Thinking Necessary in Everyday Life?

Let's imagine each detail as a specific action or event influencing others.

"One day, I was rude to my teacher. He got angry and told my parents. My parents were upset and decided not to buy me the gaming console I'd been looking forward to. In the end, my relationships with both the teacher and my parents were strained, and I ended up without the long-awaited gift."
(Christoffel, 13 years old)

In this chain of events, there are causes and effects. Some actions can be both the result of one event and the cause of another. That's why we call these connections cause-and-effect relationships.

Now, let's mentally spin Christoffel's first "gear" in the opposite direction: "One day, I complimented my teacher..."—in other words, we're changing the cause of everything that happened. How will his story change? Write it down or draw it out!

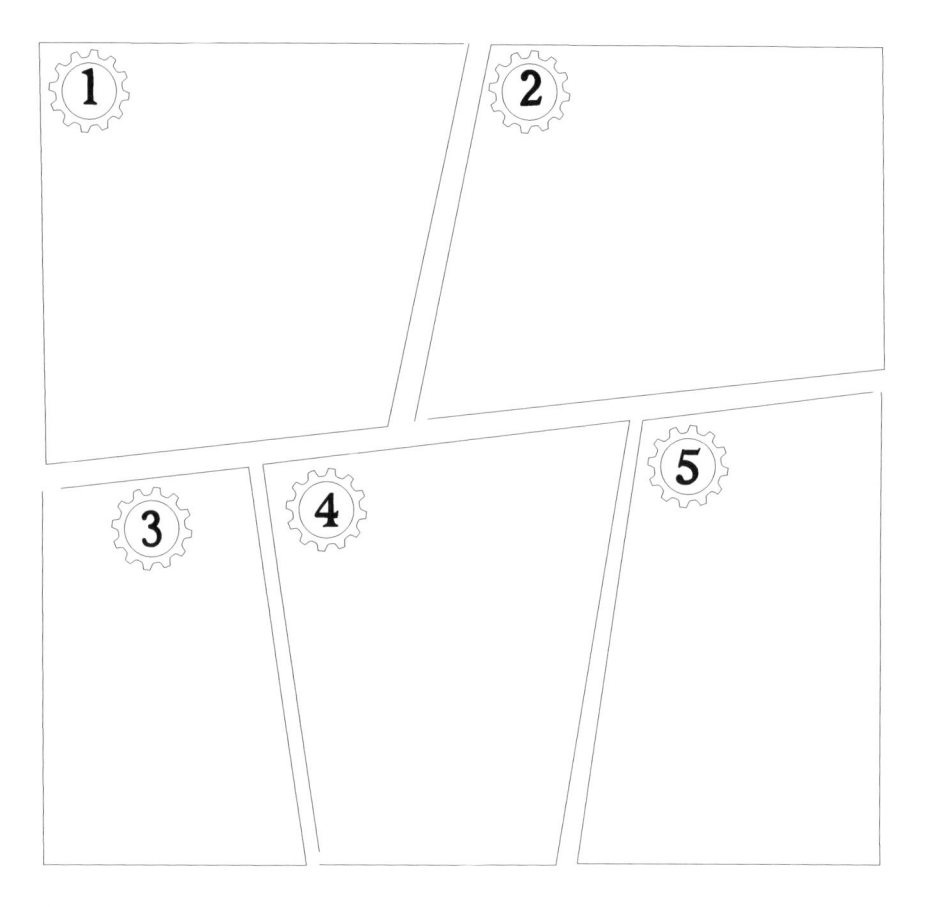

> Here you need to ask yourself two questions again:
>
> How are the different actions and events **connected**?
> How do some actions or events **influence** others?

Think of a story from your own life. Jot it down so that each action or event is a separate detail in the overall picture of what happened. It could be three, four, or as many details as you like! But try to consider the connections between them and how they influence each other!

Mentally turn the first detail in the opposite direction—imagine everything started differently. Think about how that could change the entire course of your story. Don't stop there. Try turning the second or third detail—imagine how things could have gone a different way and how that would've changed everything.

So, is systemic thinking necessary in everyday life?

○ Yes, it helps connect different events together.

○ Hmm, I haven't decided yet.

○ No way! Why would I care how things are connected?

Systemic thinking helps us build chains of events, see our behavior as a system of interconnected actions, and better understand how the things we do affect us and others. But that's not all…

What Else?

Let's say you're planning to get a birthday gift for a friend.

What's your approach?

○ Give them what they specifically asked for.

○ Buy what I would like to receive if I was in their place.

○ Try to understand what might bring them joy.

○ Reflect on how close our relationship is and how that affects my willingness to invest in the gift.

○ Consider how much time I have to choose the gift.

○ Think about whether I can afford the gift and how it will affect my expenses and financial plans.

Or _____

_____

_____

Which option has the most "gears"—details and nuances that are connected and need to be considered when choosing a gift?

The first and second options are the quickest ways to solve a problem. But are they the most effective? Sometimes, yes. Quick and simple solutions can be perfectly reasonable when dealing with familiar and straightforward tasks.

For example, in the morning, you brush your teeth while half-asleep, not really thinking about how this will impact your day or your future. And you probably aren't considering how your toothpaste affects the environment or where the leftover bits of breakfast go when you rinse them down the sink.

○ Exactly.
○ Never thought much about the purpose of this activity.
○ Or _____

But sometimes, you have to think about multiple questions at once and consider several factors at the same time, like in the third option for choosing a gift. In these cases, it makes sense to turn on your systemic thinking and carefully consider your decision from all angles.

How Do I Turn On Systemic Thinking?

With questions! See, you've already done it! Here, try to activate your systemic thinking. Spend a couple of minutes on each question and mentally explore the answers.

These questions help you see how different parts of your life are connected.

How are my savings related to my spending?

How does my diet affect my body and health?

How do the news programs I watch impact my views and emotions?

How are my grades in math connected to my grades in _____?

How is my attitude toward one person, _____
_____
related to my attitude toward another person,
_____?

These questions aren't the only way to jumpstart your systemic thinking and apply it to understand yourself and solve your problems. Don't worry, there are more methods coming up!

Long Story Short...

Systemic thinking is all about:

	X	V
Bringing order to the messy closets of your life (both literal and figurative).	☐	☐
Figuring out how one action or event impacts another.	☐	☐
Tackling problems and situations by considering all the little details and nuances.	☐	☐
Making big decisions while keeping all the different factors in mind.	☐	☐
Asking questions about how everything's connected.	☐	☐
Creating chaos inside and out.	☐	☐
Focusing only on isolated details of a situation.	☐	☐
Making quick, automatic decisions.	☐	☐

IN ONE EAR AND OUT THE OTHER... HOW DO I RETAIN WHAT I LEARN?

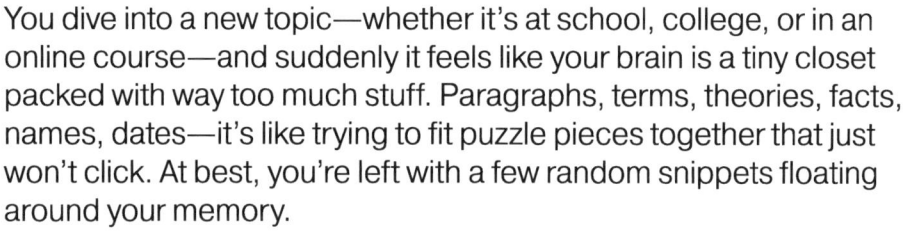

You dive into a new topic—whether it's at school, college, or in an online course—and suddenly it feels like your brain is a tiny closet packed with way too much stuff. Paragraphs, terms, theories, facts, names, dates—it's like trying to fit puzzle pieces together that just won't click. At best, you're left with a few random snippets floating around your memory.

"Yesterday, we studied Ancient Greece. The teacher told us all these cool stories about the cities and people back then, ancient philosophers, and gods. I even managed to jot everything down. But today? I can't really remember much of anything. I recall someone lived in a barrel... and Alexander the Great's horse was named Bucephalus. But that's about it." (Klim, 15)

Sound familiar?

○ A bit too familiar. ○ Yeah, that happens sometimes. ○ Nope, that's never happened to me.

So, why couldn't Klim remember everything he learned in class?

☐ Klim's history teacher must be a bore.
☐ Klim has a bad memory.
☐ Klim wasn't paying much attention.
☐ Klim slacked off and didn't write anything down.
☐ Or _____

Most of the time, remembering stuff depends on how we organize our new knowledge. You can pay attention, take notes like a champ, and still end up with a big blank. Even if the class, lecture, or textbook is fascinating, sometimes you only remember bits and pieces. It's not always about having a bad memory, losing focus, or being lazy—it's often because people aren't using the power of systemic thinking!

The Map of New Knowledge

A map is both a strategy and a system. If you're heading out on an adventure to new places, it's easy to get lost without a map. The same goes for diving into new topics. Without a special map, you can lose sight of the horizon in the sea of information. When you're learning, you need a guide—a knowledge map! It helps you organize and make sense of any information.

Organizing your knowledge is like organizing your desk. It's all about bringing order and putting everything in the right place, so writing utensils don't end up scattered and school assignments don't mysteriously go missing. You do that already, right? (Wink, wink.)

This is a topic. It's made up of different parts.

Start by writing the topic you're studying in the center of a page.
It could be a textbook chapter, a scientific theory, a historical era, or how some gadget works. Circle it.

A knowledge map is kind of like the Solar System. The Sun is in the middle, surrounded by planets, and each planet has its own moons.

It's a system that goes from the big picture to the little details: "forest—trees—branches."

1.
2.
3.
4.

This is a topic. It's made up of different parts.

Around it, jot down the main sections or blocks that make up the topic.
Try to keep it to seven blocks or fewer—trust me, your brain will thank you. Circle each one and connect them to the main topic with arrows.

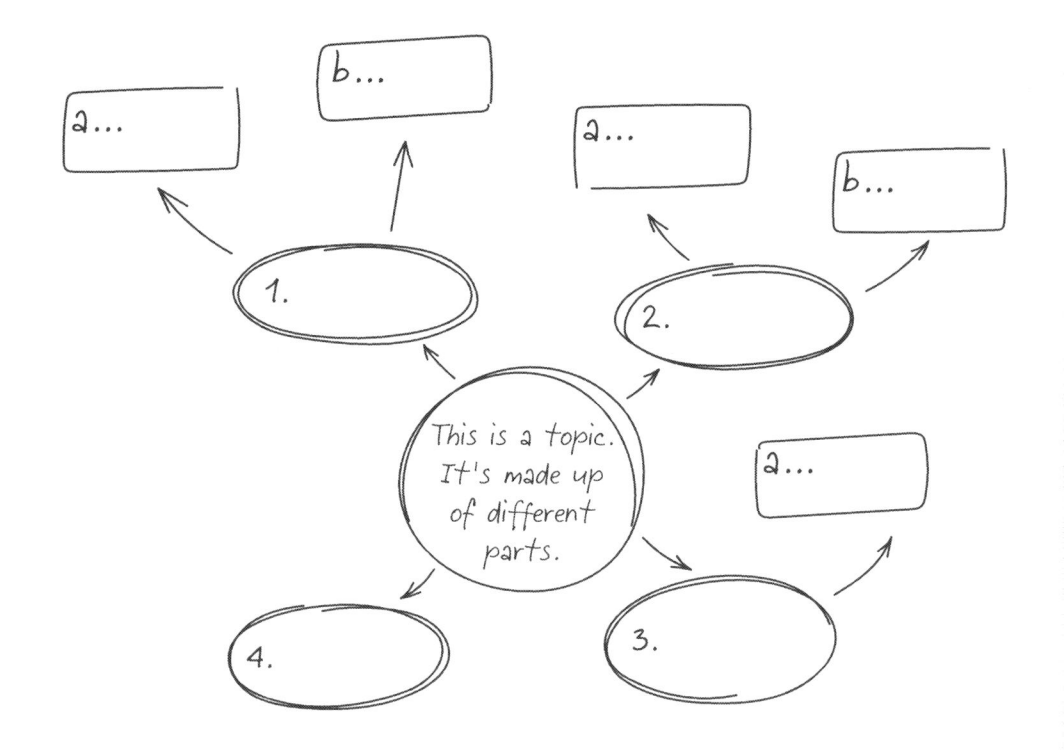

Around each section or block, write down what fits into it.
These can be questions, facts, terms—whatever you've got! Just keep it light; don't overload each section with too much stuff.

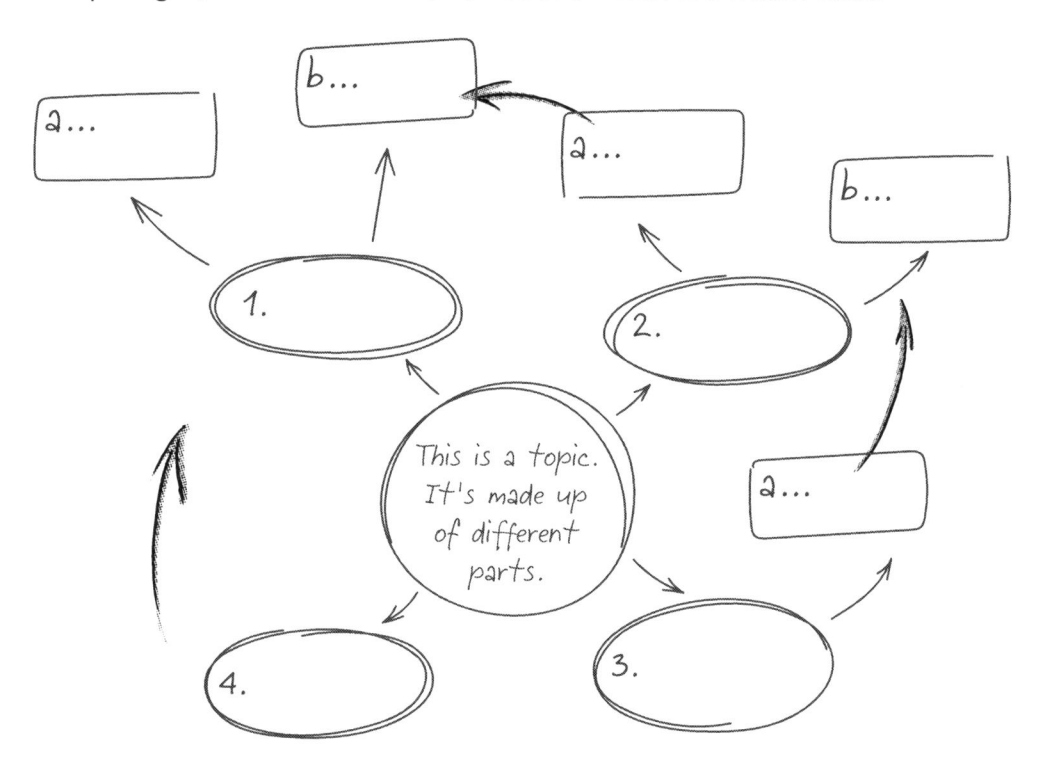

Now, check if there are extra connections between parts of your map.
These might link big sections, or connect items within a block, or even between different blocks.

Worried that creating a map like this is some epic, time-sucking task? Nah, it's actually simple and super fun. Give it a try, and you'll see for yourself!

Do you think it matters which directions the arrows point in?

175

Zombies? Again!?

Let's say you're studying zombies. You crack open your trusty Zombie-ology textbook and dive into the first chapter:

§1.1 Origins and Lifestyle of Zombies

The study of zombies begins with understanding their origins. Commonly, zombies result from zombie viruses or unsuccessful scientific experiments. Additionally, individuals can become zombies through bites from other zombies.

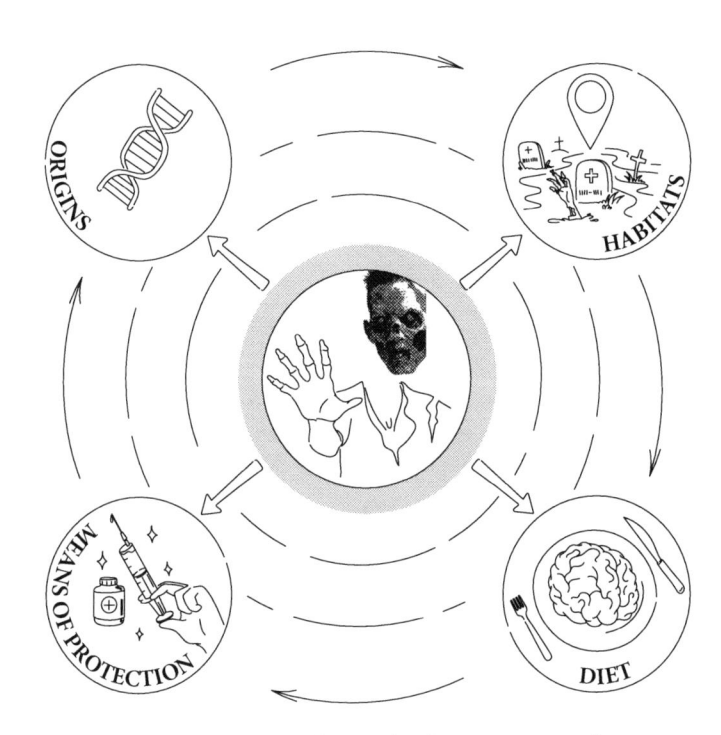

Most lectures and textbooks are all about linear thinking: step one, step two, and so on. You're expected to take in the info, understand it, and memorize it in order. But that's not always the best way to learn.

Systemic thinking breaks free from the traditional linear approach to learning, making learning new info easier and more effective.

Habitats of zombies typically include graveyards, abandoned buildings, and deserted cities. Their diet primarily consists of human brains, which makes them a significant threat. Effective strategies for protection include the development of vaccines against the zombie virus. In the event of encountering zombies, it is advisable to seek shelter in a secure location, such as a shopping mall, and possess skills such as running quickly and operating a vehicle for self-defense.

So much text to memorize, and tomorrow's the practical exam—zombie-watching in the wild. If you don't remember anything from the book, you might not make it back from that field trip... Yikes! But hey, no worries. We're going to build ourselves a killer zombie knowledge map.

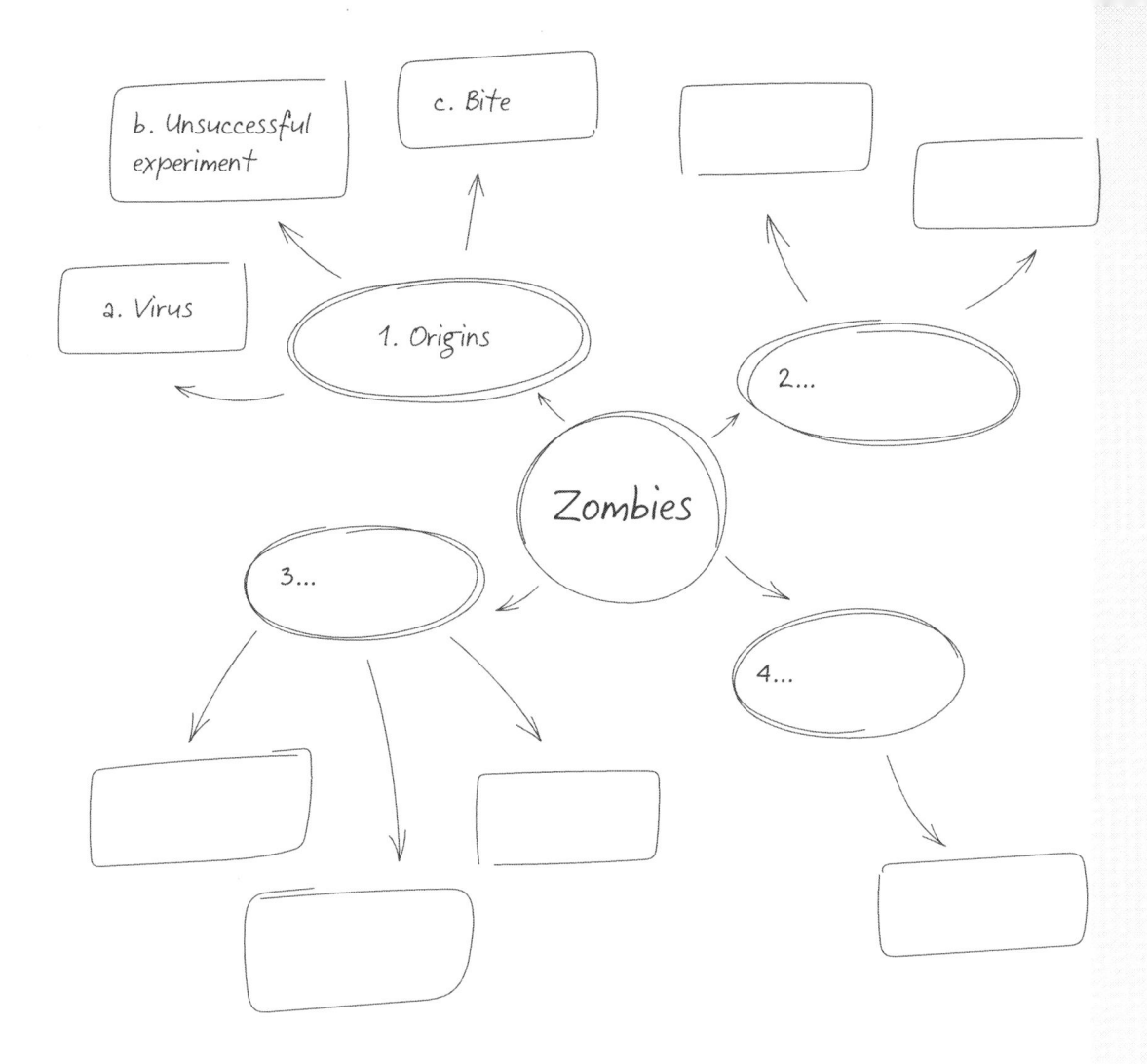

1. Origins
- a. Virus
- b. Unsuccessful experiment
- c. Bite

Zombies
- 1. Origins
- 2. ...
- 3. ...
- 4. ...

First, identify the main blocks that make up the topic. When working with text, you can <u>highlight</u> these blocks directly in the material and then transfer them to your knowledge map. Label these blocks as 1, 2, 3, and so on on your map.

◯ Done.

Next, review the textbook text again and (underline) key terms associated with each block of the topic. Transfer these terms to your map, labeling them with letters: a, b, c, and so on.

◯ Done.

Look for additional connections between elements of your map. For example, link "virus" and "vaccine" with arrows to show their relationship.

◯ Done.

By applying systemic thinking, you turn a lengthy text into a straightforward diagram. Keeping this map in mind should be a breeze—unless, of course, you're a zombie!

When working with text, mark different elements of your analysis in different ways.

In your diagram, employ different colors and types of arrows to maintain clarity and avoid making the system you created for coherence... illegible, even to you.

The Map Was Inside You All Along

When you head out for a walk in the city, do you take a map with you? If the area is familiar, you don't need a physical map—it's already in your head! The system of streets, hidden courtyards, friends' homes, favorite park benches, and lookouts with undeniable views has become a part of you.

In the same way, any new knowledge can become a part of you. How? By memorizing your knowledge map and using it regularly!

Once you've created a map for the topic you're studying, close your eyes and imagine the process of building it:

- 👁 You're staring at a blank sheet of paper.
- 👁 In the center of the page, draw the "sun"—the name of your topic.
- 👁 Place the "planets"—the major sections of the topic—around it.

What does each planet represent?

- 👁 Surrounding each section, draw the "moons"—the individual elements of this knowledge.

What do these moons contain?

- 👁 Connect the elements with arrows, like the orbits of celestial bodies.

What do these arrows signify?

From Theory to Practice!

Try it right now—draw a knowledge map for the text on the next page. Then, do it again in your mind with your eyes closed.

The topic of Ancient Greece consists of cities, myths, philosophers, and conquerors. It was made up of many city-states, with Athens and Sparta being the largest.

Greek mythology is full of stories about Zeus, Poseidon, and other gods that the ancient Greeks worshiped. Philosophy was a big deal in Greek culture, with famous thinkers like Socrates, Plato, Aristotle, and Diogenes (who lived in a barrel). And let's not forget the great warriors—like Alexander the Great, who led his army all the way to India on his horse, Bucephalus.

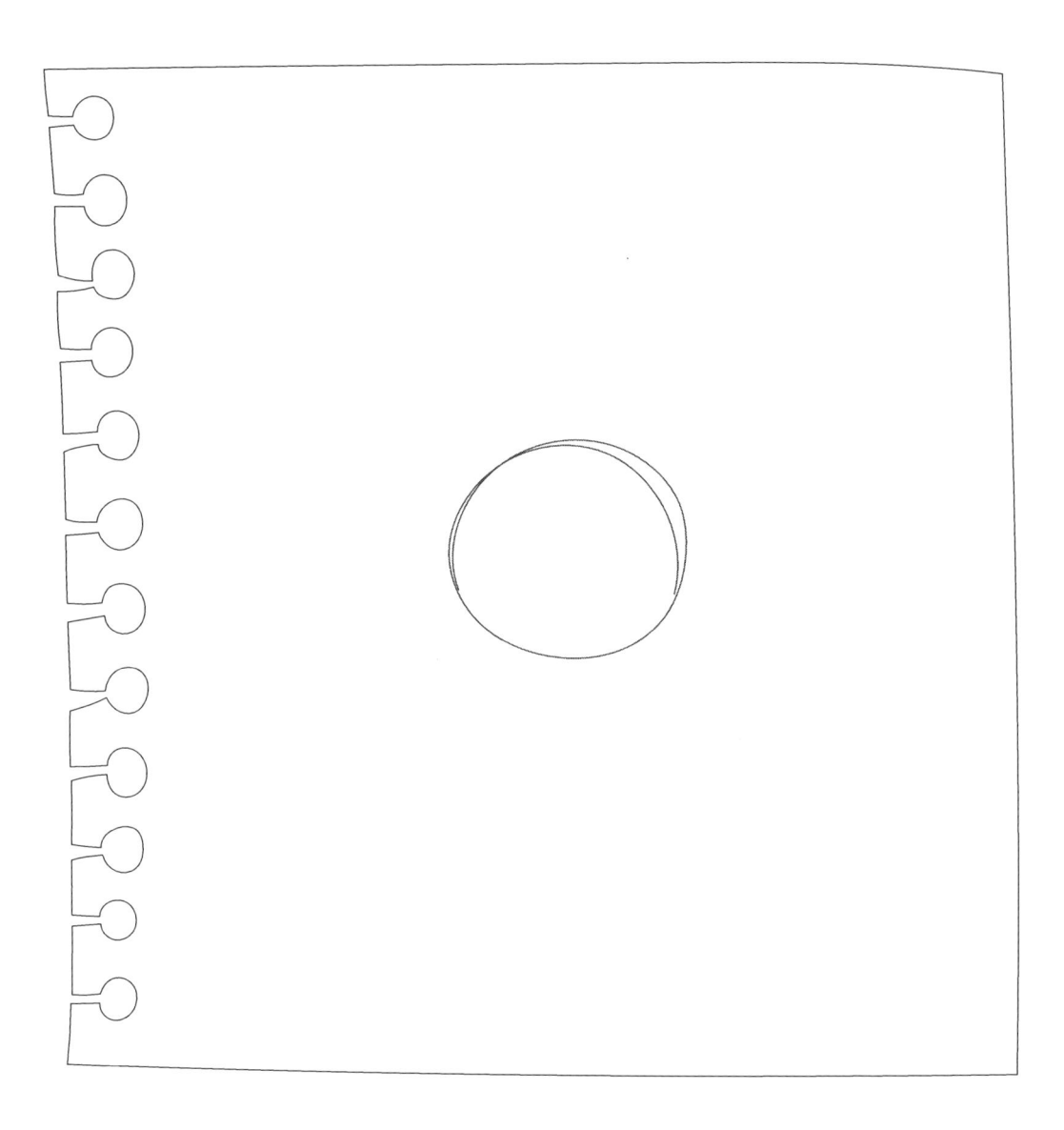

Don't forget about critical thinking if any of the facts seem odd or raise doubts.

If you're having trouble clearly visualizing the map with your eyes closed, take a look at it again and try once more. Sometimes it takes a few attempts before the map sticks in your memory. But admit it, this approach is much easier and more engaging than just cramming text!

After some time, like the next day, try drawing the map from memory. Compare it to the original and see which parts you've forgotten. Focus on those areas to improve your recall.

A knowledge map is a tool you should actively use. You can use it to explain the topic to a classmate, friend, or family member. You can also update and redraw it as you learn new things. The more you engage with your knowledge map, the sooner it will become a part of you!

So, what should I do to remember stuff better?

- [ ] Activate systematic thinking.
- [ ] Look at the new topic as a system of knowledge.
- [ ] Create a knowledge map.
- [ ] Retain the map's image in your memory.
- [ ] Use the map to explain the topic to yourself and others.

Or

- [ ] Deactivate systematic thinking.
- [ ] Chuck the new topic up to a set of unrelated facts.
- [ ] Memorize individual elements in a strict sequence.

EENY, MEENY, MINY, MOE...UGH, I CAN'T DECIDE!

Every day, we make dozens of decisions. Some are so straightforward that we don't think twice: which glass to pour water into, where to drop off our backpack, how to respond to a friend's greeting. But sometimes, decisions are more complex. At such moments, you might feel lost. You want to take action but don't know what to do. Anxiety and fear of making a mistake can paralyze you and prevent you from choosing anything.

When do you find it hardest to choose and make decisions?

- [ ] When there are too many options and possibilities.
- [ ] When the decision impacts my future.
- [ ] When I have no idea what to do.
- [ ] When I have little time to decide.
- [ ] When _____
- [ ] When _____
- [ ] When _____
- [ ] When _____

Do you wish there was some sort of blueprint for making difficult decisions? Good news: there is!

Is choosing and deciding the same thing?

Decisions are based on choices. For example, deciding where to study depends on the choice of specialty and type of educational institution. Deciding who to be friends with is based on choosing like-minded people from those around you. Deciding what to buy involves choosing between spending money and saving it. Even when it seems like there's no choice, we still choose between two alternatives: **to act** or **not to act**.

Decision-Making as Part of Something Bigger

Critical, strategic, and creative thinking set the stage for new decisions. To make specific decisions, it's often necessary to consider many details and how they interrelate. That's where systemic thinking comes in.

"At school, we could choose between several extracurriculars and clubs. Since I had limited time, I narrowed it down to two options—programming and theater. Choosing one was tough! I wanted to learn programming—I didn't know much about it, but it would be useful in the future. But I also really enjoyed performing on stage and playing different roles. If I chose theater, it would be fun and energizing. In the end, I chose programming because it's a crucial skill in today's world. Unfortunately, that took up all of my time and I had to give up theater..." (Jarome, 15 years old)

Even the simplest decisions are part of a bigger system:

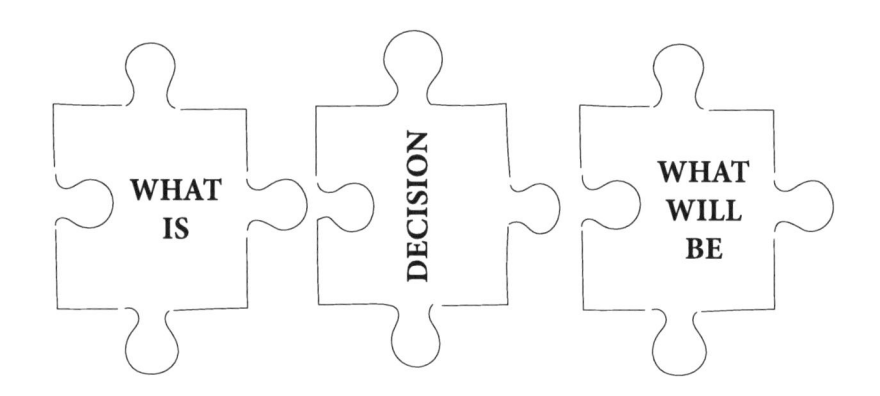

WHAT IS — DECISION — WHAT WILL BE

What were Jarome's circumstances before he made his decision?

Jarome had free time.

Jarome couldn't _____

Jarome loved _____

_____

_____

_____

When we're faced with a choice between several options, it's called a **dilemma**.

Every decision is a piece of a mosaic that forms the picture of life. Some decisions have a minor impact on the overall flow of life, while others are crucial, defining what that image will look like.

When making a decision, it's important to look not only forward but also backward—to what has happened before. This helps you understand how the decision might impact your life.

What decision specifically did Jarome make?

The results of our decisions can be positive or negative, or sometimes both at the same time. Mark which outcomes of Jarome's choice might have a positive 👍 impact on him, and which ones can't 👎.

What might the consequences of this decision be?

-- 👍 👎

-- 👍 👎

-- 👍 👎

-- 👍 👎

You can't always predict the exact outcomes of your decisions ahead of time. But it's still crucial to think about them and consider the potential results.

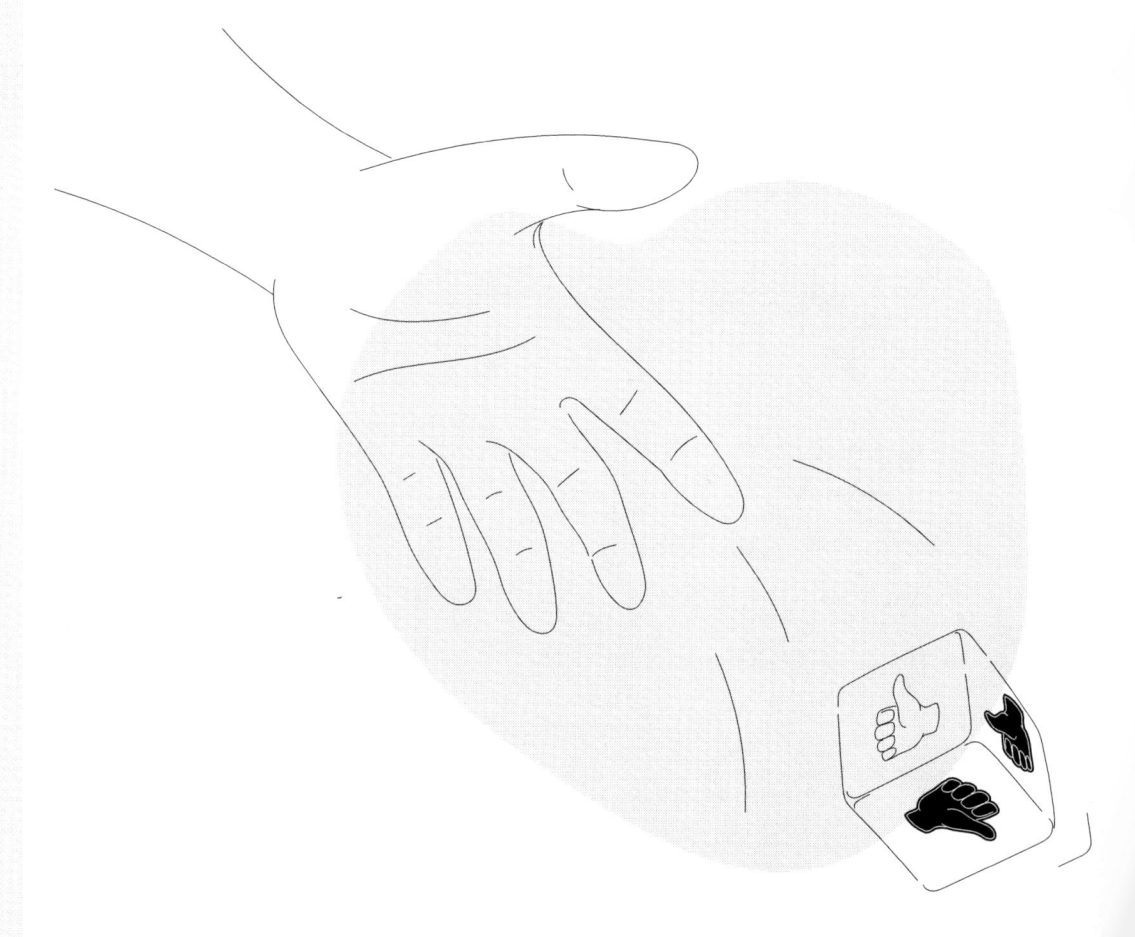

Who determines whether your decision leads to positive or negative results? Only you. And your opinion on this may differ from that of others.

Make Decisions Systematically!

When faced with a tough decision, try breaking it down systematically:

	If I choose...	If I choose...
Positive outcomes		
Negative outcomes		

When considering the results of different options, think about both the immediate and long-term outcomes—what might happen in the coming days as well as what could be down the road a year or more.

Which option might offer more positive outcomes and fewer negative ones? Perhaps that's the option to focus on.

To Act or Not to Act?

Sometimes, you have to choose between action and inaction: Should you drink the offered alcohol at a party or refuse? Should you start preparing for your exam today or tomorrow? Should you share your struggles with a close friend?

If you decide to buy a ticket to your favorite movie, you know in advance that your savings will decrease, but you'll enjoy the film.

But what if you decide to start going out with someone? It's hard to predict in advance how it will impact your life.

In such cases, try this decision-making system:

	Action	Inaction
Positive outcomes	- - - - - - - - - -	- - - - - - - - - -
Negative outcomes	- - - - - - - - - -	- - - - - - - - - -

> When something feels scary or uncomfortable, it might seem like doing nothing is the safest option. But inaction also has its consequences.

> Sometimes, getting an outside perspective can be helpful. Discuss your notes and thoughts with someone close to you. There may be pros and cons you haven't considered, but someone else might easily spot!

List the pros and cons of taking action versus doing nothing. This will give you a clear picture of the effects of each choice and help you make an informed final decision.

Simple or Complex

Decisions can be simple or complex. Simple decisions require so little effort, you could make them in your sleep! For instance:

Wearing red sneakers or black ones.

Taking the bus or the metro.

Choosing strawberry ice cream or banana.

- - - - - - - - - -

- - - - - - - - - -

- - - - - - - - - -

- - - - - - - - - -

Complex decisions require more time and effort. You need to carefully weigh all the pros and cons, compare different options, and consider how each choice might impact your life. For example:

Should I ask someone I like out on a date, or should I hold off?

Should I enroll in a math class or a language class?

Should I buy a new speaker now, or save my money for later?

- -

- -

- -

Thanks to systematic thinking, you get a holistic view of complex decisions. You gain a better understanding of how these decisions can shape or change your life. This doesn't mean every decision will be perfect. Life's picture is rarely flawless. However, even decisions that don't turn out as expected can offer valuable lessons.

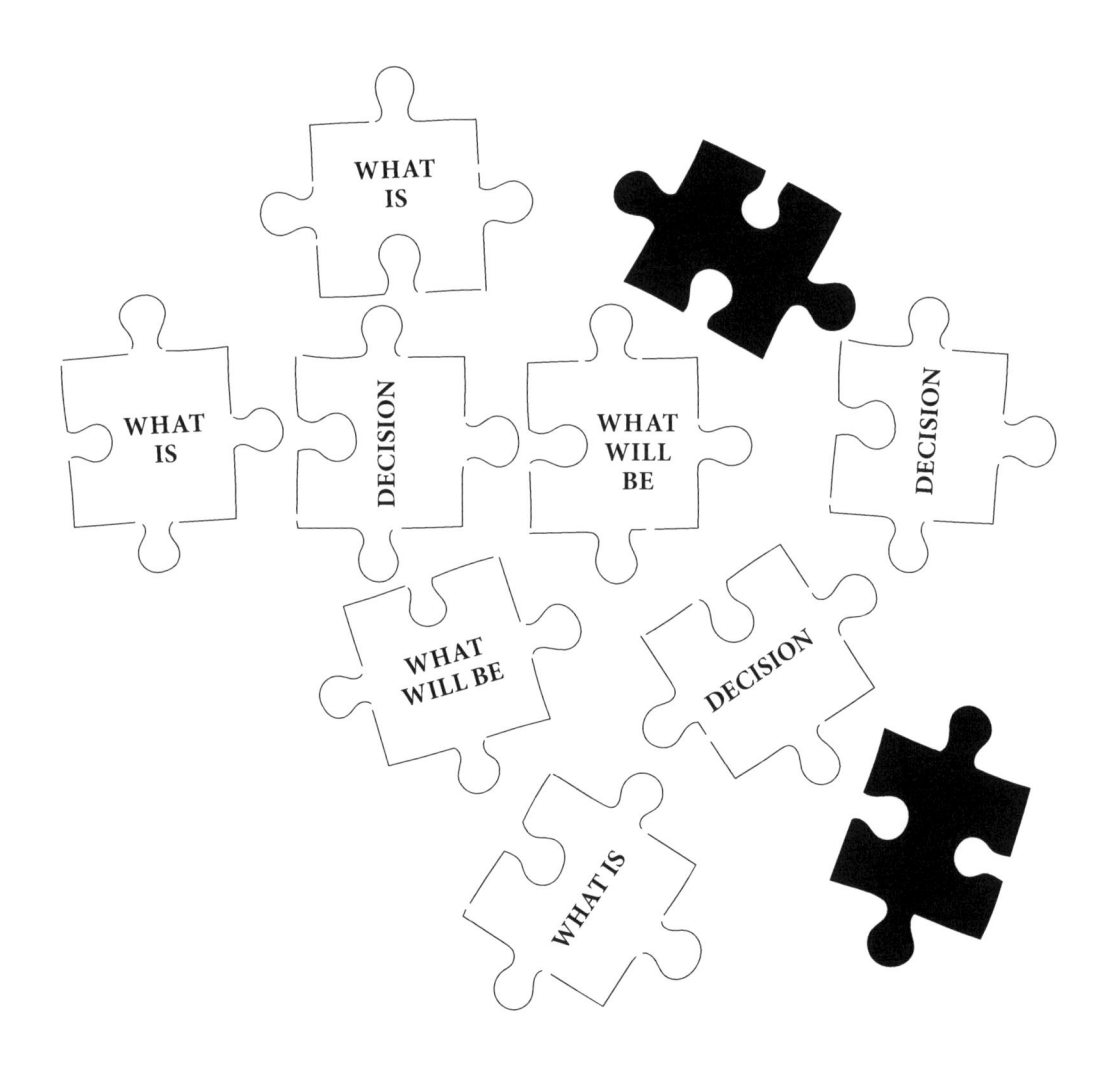

That's a Wrap!

- [ ] Every decision is part of the bigger picture of your life.
- [ ] It's always tied to a choice, sometimes a tough one.
- [ ] Even by choosing not to make a decision, you are making a decision.
- [ ] Both action and inaction can lead to various outcomes.
- [ ] These outcomes might be actualized tomorrow or much later.
- [ ] It's important to consider them in advance when making decisions.
- [ ] Not all outcomes can be predicted...
- [ ] ...So no one is immune to making mistakes.
- [ ] But these decisions are also invaluable—they provide important life lessons.

Conclusion

In today's world, information is everywhere and growing at an unprecedented rate. Every single day, people across the globe generate around 300 million terabytes of data. That's a massive amount of information, which is also fuel for your mind.

When there's too little information, you might feel like something's missing, craving more news, experiences, or insights. But when there's too much, it can lead to overwhelm and confusion. It's easy to get lost in the flood of data and struggle to distinguish what's truly valuable from meaningless noise.

That's where the power of focused thinking and effective tools come in. Throughout this workbook, you've explored various strategies and techniques to manage and make sense of this flood of information. Phew, what a workout for your brain!

But don't rush to throw in the towel. As you move forward, some of these tools and techniques may become even more relevant as you face new challenges and opportunities. You'll find that being able to strategically apply different types of thinking can make a significant difference.

Remember, thoughtful decisions and effective use of your mental tools will continuously refine and develop your mind. You now have a clear understanding of when and how to use different thinking strategies. Embrace this newfound capability and use it to navigate your journey ahead. Your ability to think critically, creatively, and strategically is your superpower—make the most of it!

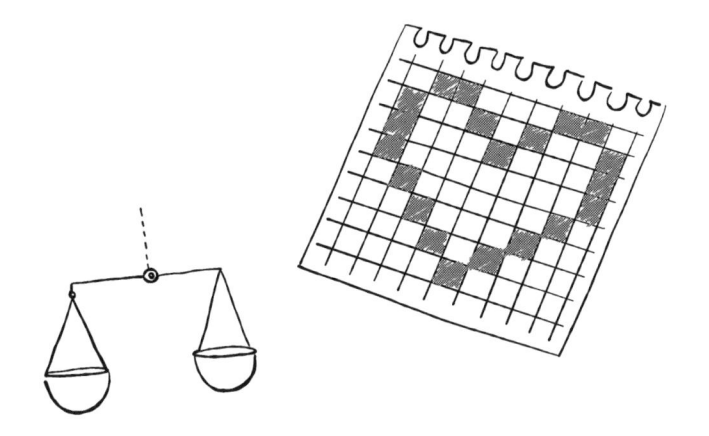

LIST OF SOURCES USED

Bailey, Chris. *Hyperfocus: How to Manage Your Attention in a World of Distraction.* Alpina Publisher, 2019.

Galef, Julia. *The Scout Mindset: Why Some People See Things Clearly and Make Better Decisions.* Mann, Ivanov & Ferber, 2021.

Goleman, Daniel. *Focus: The Hidden Driver of Excellence.* Corpus, 2017.

Grant, Adam. *Think Again: The Power of Knowing What You Don't Know.* Mann, Ivanov & Ferber, 2021.

Dennett, Daniel. *Intuition Pumps and Other Tools for Thinking.* Corpus, 2021.

Dobelli, Rolf. *The Art of Thinking Clearly.* Mann, Ivanov & Ferber, 2014.

Micalco, Michael. *Thinker Toys: 21 Ideas to Foster Creative Thinking.* Mann, Ivanov & Ferber, 2021.

Namakonov, Igor. *Creativity: 31 Ways to Make Your Brain Work.* Alpina Publisher, 2023.

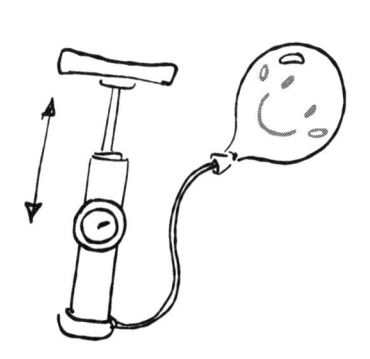

Nepryakhin, Nikolay. *Anatomy of Fallacies: The Big Book on Critical Thinking.* Alpina Publisher, 2023.

Petrocelli, David. *The Art of Spotting Bullshit: How to Avoid Being Misled and Make Better Decisions.* Bombora, 2022.

Silvanovich, Sergey. *Creative for Business: Managing Your Company's Creative Potential.* Grevcov Publishing House, 2007.

Walker, Richard. *With Eyes Wide Open: 131 Ways to See the World Differently and Find Joy in the Everyday.* Mann, Ivanov & Ferber, 2021.

Halpern, Diane. *Critical Thinking Psychology.* Peter, 2000.

Chatfield, Tom. *Critical Thinking: Analyze, Question, Form Your Own Opinions.* Alpina Publisher, 2024.

Sirdeshpande, Ranjit. *Good News: Why the World is Not as Bad as You Think.* Wren & Rook, 2021.— Winchester: Wren & Rook, 2021.

Soft skills, strong foundation

Teaching teens social-emotional skills for a great life

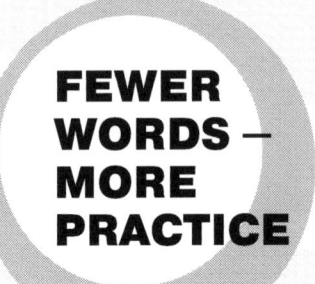

FEWER WORDS — MORE PRACTICE

Life Skills 101

A colorful, practical, and engaging guide with a workbook to practice essential soft skills every teen needs for a happier future. Fewer words—more meaning for a brighter tomorrow!

Emotions for Teens and Tweens

The first visual book on emotional intelligence for tweens and teens and a workbook with 100+ exercises and practices to help them build resilience, mental health, and master their emotions.

Relationships for Teens and Tweens

The first and only visual guide to building genuine relationships for a happier life, featuring real-life examples and 100+ practices to reinforce relationship knowledge and communication skills.

FEWER WORDS — MORE MEANING

Mastermind. The decision-making visual guide for teens and tweens

Maximize your decision-making skills by pairing the workbook with Mastermind: The Decision-Making Visual Guide for Teens and Tweens—the perfect blend of theory and practice to develop all types of thinking and make smarter choices.

THE DECISION-MAKING VISUAL GUIDE

MASTERMIND

FOR TEENS & TWEENS

FEWER WORDS — MORE MEANING

My notes

My notes

My notes

My notes

Popular science publication for middle and high school students

THE THINKER'S TOOLBOX:
Mastering Decisions Workbook for Teens & Tweens

Idea Author and Editor-in-Chief: *Maria Gorina*
Text Author: *Igor Pavlov*
Prepress: *Ekaterina Aleksashkina*
Language Editor: *Sofiya Ivanova*

All rights to the illustrations belong to Ivigreen LLC.

For more information contact:
hello@ivigreen.com

ivigreen.com

Made in United States
Orlando, FL
29 March 2025